A JUZ A DAY

Summary of the Quran

A Juz A Day: Summary of the Quran

First published in Malaysia by:
Tertib Publishing
23-2 Jalan PJS 5/30
Petaling Jaya Commercial City (PJCC)
46150 Petaling Jaya, Selangor
Malaysia

Tel: +603 7772 3156

First Edition: June 2019
Second Edition: August 2019
Third Edition: May 2020

Cataloguing in-Publication Data is available from the National

Library of Malaysia
ISBN: 978-967-2420-25-5

Cover design: Miza Mumtaz
Transcription: Faslin Syarina Salim
Typesetting & Layout: Inda Hayati Samsi
Printed by: Firdaus Press Sdn. Bhd.

CONTENT

PREFACE

The Qur'an is not a storybook of wondrous tales and ancient fables, isolated from the realities and complexities of real life. Each verse—in fact, each letter—is miraculously precise in meaning, succinct in message and pure in sound.

The life lessons that may be derived from the Qur'an are infinite. The more one contemplates it, approaching it with a sincere heart and giving it one's full attention while recognising its magnificence, the more one's heart connects with The Almighty.

Although it is impossible to articulate a translation that clearly establishes the majestic nature of the Qur'an in any language of the world, nevertheless, Muslims need to become more familiar with the overall coherence of its message in their native language.

During *taraweeh*, myself and other *imams* will lead the congregation in prayer, beginning on the first night with the opening chapter of the Qur'an and we finish it insha'Allah, before the end of the blessed month of Ramadan.

The aim of this work before you is to highlight key themes and messages of the Qur'an that will be recited each night so that those who are not able to understand the Arabic reading can feel a connection with what they will hear that evening in the prayers, by reading this summation.

The Qur'an refers to a wealth of human experience, seeking to enrich our lives on earth before our eventual return to our Maker, the Most High.

The Prophet (s.a.w.) was commanded to follow his righteous predecessors and take heed from their trials and inspiration from their eventual and divinely ordained triumph.

Allah, the Most High, instructs us to contemplate the final Word and benefit from its lessons and parables:

وَلَقَدْ صَرَّفْنَا فِى هَـٰذَا ٱلْقُرْءَانِ لِلنَّاسِ مِن كُلِّ مَثَلٍ ۚ وَكَانَ ٱلْإِنسَـٰنُ أَكْثَرَ شَىْءٍ جَدَلًا ۝

And We have certainly diversified in this Qur'an for the people from every [kind of] example; but man has ever been, most of anything, [prone to] dispute. [Surah Al-Kahf, 18:54]

I pray that the Qur'an remains a light for us in the darkness of excess and that it leads us to the moderate, straight path of righteousness. I pray that we practice it faithfully by day and busy ourselves with its recitation by night.

May Allah grant us its guidance and guide others to it through us.

In need of your sincere du'a,

Imam Yahya A Ibrahim

JUZ 1

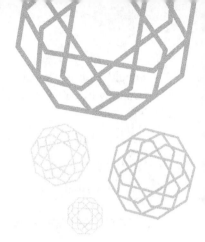

This is the greatest chapter of the Qur'an. It is the essence of all of Islam. In the first half of the *surah*, Allah (s.w.t.) magnifies Himself, praises Himself; and in the second half, He speaks about our need to develop sincerity and worship of Him. He speaks about the reality of guidance for us in life as being an avoidance of misguidance, which He warns us about. True guidance comes from Allah. It is something we have to ask Him for, and we then demonstrate our viability of practising what has been received by us. Therefore, the root of guidance is to put into practise the knowledge we have. Allah then juxtaposes that by giving us the reality of misguidance.

He speaks about misguidance in two ways. There are those who anger Him (referring to those who have knowledge but do not practice it), and then there are those who have been misguided and have left upon a path of deviance (referring to those who practise and have good intentions, but do not have knowledge). These misguided do not follow the spirit of revelation. These are the two warnings at the end of Surah Al-Fatihah, where we ask Allah to protect us from those who anger Him, in reference to those who have knowledge and do not practise it, and those who have been left astray—the ones who try to do what is right but do not have the knowledge and do not reach where they should be with Allah.

The *du'a* we make at the end of the *surah*, "*Guide us to the straight path—the path of those upon whom You have bestowed favour, not of those who have evoked [Your] anger or of those who are astray,*" is as if confirmed in the opening of the second chapter of the Qur'an, in Surah Al-Baqarah (The Cow) when He says, "*This is the Book about which there is no doubt...*".

Surah Al-Baqarah is the longest chapter of the Qur'an. It is the chapter where the Prophet (s.a.w.) said that for the one who masters it and practises it, the Qur'an will speak on their behalf on the Day of Judgement. It has in it the greatest verse of the Qur'an, which is Ayatul Kursi. This verse is read as spiritual protection and as assistance when seeking Allah's help. This *surah* also contains the greatest two verses that can provide protection from any fear. The Prophet (s.a.w.)

said that these two last verses of Surah Al-Baqarah are enough for everything; it will suffice for us against the many difficulties we face. They are treasures from the throne of Allah (s.w.t.).

Allah (s.w.t.) begins the *surah* by mentioning that the Qur'an comes from *Alif Lam Mim*, disjointed letters in Arabic that miraculously have been chosen by Allah to give us a coherent message. The *surah*'s overarching theme is about devotion and submission to the message of God that is received through revelation without question. Even when it goes against some of the base desires, animalistic instincts and urges that one has, the spirit behind revelation is to make a person the most complete human being there is. From there we can observe that those who strayed away from submitting to a path of truth and from devotion from Allah, are highlighted in the Qur'an for it.

For example, in the story of Adam (a.s.), Allah said, "*Do not go near this tree.*" It is an instruction. It does not matter what the tree is, whether it is lawful or not; that is not the point. The instruction is to not come near the tree. In the story of the cow (which is where the *surah* gets its name), the Israelites were asked to slaughter a cow and they began to question: what colour was it, where can they find it, how much was it worth, on and on. Instead of just slaughtering a cow as Allah had instructed, the more they increased in their questioning of Allah, and as a result, Allah made it more stringent upon them.

When we juxtapose the two stories of Adam (a.s.) and the cow at the beginning of Surah Al-Baqarah, with the story of Iblis who was also given instructions by Allah to bow down, give his service to and be subjugated to Adam (a.s.), Iblis' reply was, *I'm better than him. I'm not going to follow the revelation. I won't follow the instruction. I'm going to do what I think rather than what Allah has commanded.* These elements in this first *juz* are what essentially make up the first twenty pages of the chapter.

Surah Al-Baqarah then highlights three categories of people: the believers (*al-mu'minun*), those who choose to disbelieve (*al-kafirun*) and those who hide their disbelief and pretend to be faithful (the hypocrites, *al-munafiqun*). In the midst of that, Allah (s.w.t.) gives warnings to nations, peoples and tribes, collectively and spiritually. Allah then tells us through the Qur'an that the nations that were destroyed before us was a result of them having lost their way. It also hardened their hearts because they developed rancour to the spirit of revelation. Whenever they were asked to do something, whenever messengers were sent, they would rebel against them. They belied the messengers and would not accept them as true.

Ibrahim (a.s.) is referenced at the beginning, the middle, and the end of Surah Al-Baqarah. Allah (s.w.t.) describes Ibrahim (a.s.) and Isma'il (a.s.) as being those who heard Allah and obeyed Him. The name *Isma'il* comes from the word '*Sami'Allah*'—the one who hears the invocation of Allah. They did as they were instructed. When Ibrahim (a.s.) was told to leave his family in the desert—*I would do as instructed.* When Ibrahim (a.s.) was asked to build this foundation as a back up to a Kaabah—*I would do as instructed.* When Isma'il (a.s.) was told to be patient when Ibrahim (a.s.) said *I will slaughter you*—*I would do as instructed.* They were therefore given as examples of those who follow the spirit of revelation.

Finally, righteousness is not inherited. Ibrahim (a.s.) made *du'a* to Allah that the rest of his progeny will be protected and have the covenant of Allah. Righteousness is not inherited by lineage but belongs to those who are truly devout.

The *juz* then ends with the children of Ibrahim (a.s.) making the same plea to Allah (s.w.t.), due to their deep concern and worry about their future generations. They questioned them, "*What will you worship after I am gone?*" Their reply was "*We shall worship your God and the God of your fathers, Ibraham, Isma'il (a.s.), and Ishaq—one single God.*"

That is the hope that you and I have for our future generations. At the end of this *juz*, Allah (s.w.t.) makes us understand that, although nothing is guaranteed except our good deeds which we make purely intended for the sake of Allah, what we do now in our devotion and adherence to revelation *will* have an impact our future progeny and generations.

JUZ 2

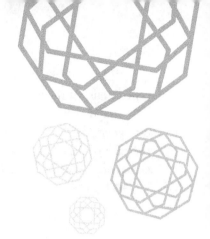

Allah (s.w.t.) begins the *juz* by speaking about the *qiblah*, the direction of prayer. And He speaks about it in such a way to address the contention that was being made by other faith communities in Madinah, particularly the Jews, who argued as to why the Prophet (s.a.w.) had turned the direction of the *qiblah* back to Makkah, rather than Jerusalem.

The Prophet (s.a.w.) was instructed by Allah to respond by telling them that this has always been the intention of the *qiblah*—that the oldest house, the first place of worship has always been Makkah Al-Mukarramah, and it is here that the greatest ancestry of humanity in terms of their faithfulness and worship began. None would despise this place unless there is a problem within their hearts, as it is a beautiful place with a beautiful environment.

The *qiblah* is also seen as a place of moderation. It is not a place that is meant to subdue anyone. And it is not meant to be that, unless you follow it, you cannot have any faithfulness. In fact, Allah speaks about purity here, which is the third theme. Purity in the heart is more important than the direction of the prayer. *Wherever you turn, you will find Allah's Face present to receive your prayers.* But moderation is spoken of in the two extremes of love and hate. Never love anything too much that you love them in a way that only Allah should be loved. And never hate anything in a way that makes you incapable of honouring them and loving them in the future. It is the eternal message in the early section of the *juz.*

Allah then transitions and speaks about *sabr* (patience). He tells us that we are going to be tested in all aspects of our lives—in wealth, in prosperity, in health, in our family, in our happiness, in our faithfulness. But the outcome is that good news is given to those who remain enduring with patience. There is fruit to that. There is something that will come out of that hardship, which is that they will find their happiness in this life and find contentment in the next life. This is one of the great and profound statements in the Qur'an—that with patience, you can find happiness and contentment here in this world even during hardship. And you will find our reward waiting in the *akhirah.*

The next statement is the concept of *siyam* (fasting or abstinence). *Siyam* is one of those great mysteries of life. It is something that has been done by the very earliest of humanity from the time of Adam (a.s.). He was ordered to fast from that tree. *Don't go to that tree, don't eat from its fruit.* It is one of those acts of worship that also encompasses other elements of worship and self-control. When fasting, you have to pray; you have to be devout; you have to control your mouth; you have to control what you say, what you do, what you see, what you hear. It is something that raises your spirit. *Perhaps you can ascend to piety*—which will become one of the great themes of this *juz* after the transition from patience. So the rules and the spirit of fasting are outlined in these verses.

Soon after, Allah speaks about *hajj*. In these verses, Allah speaks about *hajj* in terms of its rituals, not about spirituality. The spirituality aspect of *hajj* is addressed in another chapter called Surah Al-Hajj. But here is where the rules of *hajj*—the citing of the days and what you do on which particular day, when you descend from 'Arafah—are spoken of in great detail, teaching the *ummah* the rituals of *hajj*.

Then there is the transition to family law. Allah gives this topic a great deal of attention. He speaks about family law in terms of marriage and divorce. Who to marry, who not to marry, who is eligible for divorce, who should be divorced, who you should try to reconcile with, the processes of reconciliation—bringing a conciliator from his side and her side, and if they wish to rectify, Allah will help that process. Allah speaks about remarriage, widowhood, bereavement, death and also life after divorce—all of these different things. Allah speaks about paternity, child-rearing and breastfeeding laws. All of them are included in this important section, which shows that Allah looks into great detail when concerning this eternal process of family. All of that is on the backdrop of *taqwa*, fearing God and being obedient in conscience to Him. With *taqwa*, this God-consciousness, we will have fear of any oppression that we may cause and bring upon others.

Allah then transitions from that to a real-life demonstration of it through the story of Dawud (a.s.) and Jalut (David and Goliath). Allah speaks about oppression in the fame of Jalut, and then of those who are weak and disadvantaged. It is almost as if there is a paradox—similar to having a wife and children. We might be a tyrant and think we are controlling them now, but remember that there is always going to come a day of vengeance for those who are cast down. Therefore, be good with your family, your husband, your wife, and your children.

Dawud (a.s.) and Jalut is the eternal struggle of good versus evil, of weakness that ascends to supremacy, and power on account of conviction and faith. And Allah speaks about the importance of remaining patient. "*Our Lord, pour upon us patience and plant firmly our feet and give us victory over the disbelieving people.*" Patience is then juxtaposed to hastiness, to illustrate how the latter leads to destruction. When the people who were with Dawud were spoken to, they said, *Yes, of course we will fight for the truth.* But when they were confronted with the small test—to not drink from the Jordan river, except one hand—many of them could not be patient, many of them were washed away with insincerity. It is only the few, and the virtuous who are delivered victory.

That is the message to our *ummah* today. In the days of darkness that we see, if you remain firm, keep the course, purify your heart, raise your spirituality and look after what is more important; then know that the most difficult and strict of things will bring about the best causes.

That is how Juz 2 ends. The next *juz* will begin with Ayatul Kursi in the first few verses. ✺

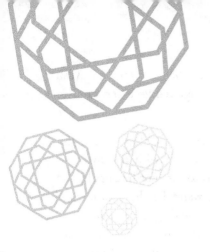

JUZ 3

This *juz* begins with the greatest verse of the Qur'an, Ayatul Kursi. This particular verse also mentions Allah's greatest names, Al-Hayy and Al-Qayyum.

Immediately after Ayatul Kursi, Allah speaks about three important stories, one after another without a break between them. The first story is about Ibrahim (a.s.) and Namrod—a man who thought he had a power that nobody could surpass, a man who thought he could give life and death. Ibrahim (a.s.) challenged Namrod and asked him to bring the sun from the west, instead of it rising from the east. He was unable to do so.

The next story is of Al-Uzayr. He is one of the prophets of Allah who came and saw the destruction of Baitul Maqdis. He exclaimed, "How can this city be brought back to life? It was thriving with faith and now it has been destroyed by these aggressors." Allah put him to death for a hundred years, and when he woke up, Allah showed him that the city had reignited itself and came to faith.

The third story is once again the story of Ibrahim (a.s.). He asked Allah to show him with his own eyes how He would bring the dead to life; not because he did not have faith but because he wanted to have an instinct in his heart that will solidify it with greater *iman*. Allah told him to take some birds, cut them into pieces, scatter them on various mountain tops and then call the birds back to him. They came back intact, as a sign of Allah's ability.

Soon after that Allah speaks about charity. This is to show us that He, Allah, is the one who is in control of everything. He brings the dead to life, He controls that which is animate and inanimate, and He is the one who can bring from where we think is nothingness, something. Therefore, do not look at our money in the way that *shaytan* seeks to frame it. *Shaytan* invites us and calls us to a belief that wealth will be deprived when we share it. Allah is the one who holds us to His generosity and being. Allah is the one who will give us greater than what we have given.

Then Allah begins to speak about financial responsibility. Once again, He speaks about the deadliness of *riba*, the immorality of usury, and the disagreeable practice of pinning under people who had borrowed from our wealth.

Allah speaks about charity and giving people good loans. Being generous in charity is one thing, but also being generous in loaning people money and expecting its return also earns you a spiritual blessing and an increase in the *barakah* that you have been provided.

The longest verse in the Qur'an, which is at the second last page of Surah Al-Baqarah, is the verse that commands us to write down all of our financial transactions and bring witnesses to it. Therefore, financial issues have great precedence in Surah Al-Baqarah.

After the last two verses of Surah Al-Baqarah, there is the transition into Surah Ali 'Imran, highlighting that the *sahabah* passed the test. The message within Surah Al-Baqarah is to submit unquestionably to Allah. Allah also promises He will never bear a soul more than it can withstand. Those last two verses of Surah Al-Baqarah are the greatest sources of protection for the believers when they recite it with that intention.

The third chapter of the Qur'an, Surah Ali 'Imran, begins with Allah's greatest names, Al-Hayy and Al-Qayyum. In a hadith of the Prophet (s.a.w.), it is mentioned that these names of Allah are found in Surah Al-Baqarah, Ali 'Imran and Taha. Therefore, the *'ulama* assume that Al-Hayy and Al-Qayyum are a reference to these greatest names because those two words in parallel are found nowhere else in the Qur'an except in those three *surah*s.

This *surah* begins with it being referred to as Al-Furqan. *The Qur'an was sent as a criterion, as a veil between right and wrong, as a separation of truth and falsehood.*

Soon after that, Allah speaks about the people of Bani Isra'il by mentioning His favour upon their ancestry. Allah speaks about the mother of Maryam (a.s.) and refers to her story of asking Allah for a child in a miraculous way. She was old and no longer of child-bearing age. She asks, *I just want one more, o' Allah, because I want to dedicate the child in service to you, to be the inheritor of his father 'Imran, to be a prophet of God.* When she later discovered that the baby was a female, it was almost as if she looked down on it. Then Allah says, *Don't you understand that a man could never reach the level of a female?*

Through the story of the mother of Maryam, it also shows the hope for the future, for us to try to be of those persons who look forward and not just beneath our feet.

Allah then transitions into a discussion about the importance of understanding that faithfulness is Islam. It is submission to Allah. It is not the word Islam as a religion, but it is the concept of submission to Allah, that the only thing accepted by God is submission to Him. That was the submission of Musa (a.s.), 'Isa (a.s.), all of the patriarchs and prophets who preceded Prophet Muhammad (s.a.w.). They all called to one thing: *tawhid*.

Allah continues in this segue when He tells us to not be from those who have this concept that anyone who is different from you is not righteous. *You will see, o' Muhammad, and o' nation in your dealings, that there are people from Bani Isra'il, people from the people of the book—the Jews and the Christians—who, if you were to give them an amount of money and ask them to return it, they are trustworthy and noble. Then there are others from amongst them who, if you were to give them greater or less, they would betray you.* Meaning, do not generalise. Not everyone is the same. If we do not want to be stereotyped, we should not do the same.

Allah ends the *juz* by discussing *Rabbaniyyin*—for us to be Godly in our conduct, to be from among those who seek to please Allah, putting ourselves in a state where we seek to take on the divine traits of Allah in our lives. For example, being *rahman* or merciful—as we seek Allah to be Ar-Rahman, the Most Merciful, towards us, be kind and merciful towards others if we want that mercy from Allah.

JUZ 4

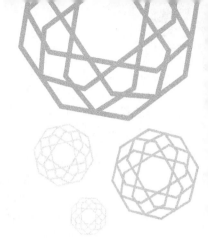

Allah (s.w.t.) begins Juz 4, which is nearer the middle-end of Surah Ali 'Imran, by speaking about the oldest place of worship—the first house that was dedicated as a place and sanctuary of worship, in the valley of Makkah.

He then continues by saying, "*Hold firmly to the rope of Allah.*" The rope of Allah is the Qur'an (i.e. revelation), and holding on to it means that we believe there is a communication from The Almighty to us on this earth to instil in us goodness. We are the best of nations if we are able to maintain our faith, enjoin what is good, and forbid what is evil. This shows us the importance of being a person who tries to bring good, not just to our own selves, but to broader elements in society.

Allah also warns us about treachery and hypocrisy—to be careful with those who try to divide and pull us apart, and who influence us not to obey leadership. This is one of the underpinnings of treachery in society and brings about a defeatist spirit.

The Almighty also speaks in detail about the Battle of Uhud, the second greatest battle of Islam. Allah tells us about the consequences of disobeying Him and disobeying His Messenger (s.a.w.)—especially in directives and orders that should make sense to us, but we instead do as our heart desires, as we are searching for the *dunya*, for that contentment of the worldly life, rather than for the *akhirah*.

Next, Allah speaks about humiliation as being directly sourced from deviance and disobedience to revelation. He tells us about the characteristics of piety to offset against that. Those who are going to bring success, who are chased and run, and who are foremost in seeking the forgiveness of their Lord—they all have particular traits. They are those who give in charity whether they are wealthy or whether they are in austere measures, and they restrict their anger and hold it within themselves. And they are capable of pushing that anger completely out of their hearts in their forgiveness and pardon of others. Surely Allah loves those who do righteousness among others.

Allah (s.w.t.) also speaks about having that defeatist, self-imposed prison of lack of success, where a person assumes that they will never be successful. *Do not ever think you will not be successful. You will ascend if you believe in yourself and you committed to faith—if you have that faithfulness in Allah.*

Allah then speaks about the greatest struggle, which is the struggle with you against yourself. That is a pretext of being able to struggle in the path of God to free those who are oppressed or who find themselves in difficulty. That is one of the greatest lessons learned from the Battle of Uhud. It was not about standing in a struggle against the oppressors and the disbelievers. Instead, it was a struggle against themselves. And then when some of the *sahabah* failed to stay on the mountain as instructed, they lost a share of the *dunya*. However, they gained the *akhirah* with Allah (s.w.t.) on account of their love for Prophet Muhammad (s.a.w.).

The *surah* then speaks about how to recover, and that Allah (s.w.t.) must be the centre of our affection and love and the target of our prayers. In the last ten verses of the *surah*, from verse 190 to 200, He begins to describe that the creation of the heavens and the earth and the alternation of night and day are signs to those who have faith and think about Allah. They are committed to God and thinking of Him in all moments of their lives—

standing, sitting, and laying down. These last ten verses were recited by the Prophet (s.a.w.) in the depths of the night and whenever he woke up from his sleep. Try to make it a *sunnah* in your life.

Allah then begins the next chapter of the Qur'an, Surah An-Nisa', which is the fourth chapter and one of the long *surah*s of the Qur'an. From the outset, Allah addresses oppression and begins to chastise those who commit oppression. He further declares that He would give victory to those who are oppressed, meaning those who are weak unto themselves, those who are abused, orphaned, and widowed—in particular, those who were prevented from being able to make *hijrah* to the Prophet Muhammad (s.a.w.).

And then Allah gives an example from real-life conditions, which is inheritance. At that time, women were completely annexed, and they themselves were inherited by future consecutive governors. Allah changes all this and puts an end to that oppression, in addition to giving women a share in the inheritance. That share of the women's inheritance is determined by Him—not by us, based on who we like and who we dislike. This helps to remove family feuds and oppression that we may cause upon each other.

Allah also gives women emancipation—an entitlement to own property, to buy, to sell, to choose whom they wish to marry, and so on. That was deemed revolutionary at that moment in history.

Finally, at the end of the *surah*, Allah speaks about the importance of *maharim*—who you are allowed and not allowed to marry—as well as clarifying all issues and details that relate to paternity.

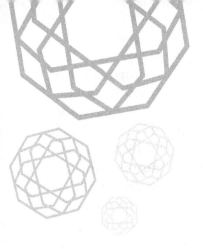

JUZ 5

Juz 5 starts near the beginning of Surah An-Nisa'. This *surah*, as mentioned in the previous *juz*, deals directly about families and women, and the oppressed is an overarching theme throughout. Taking centre stage are issues that relate to family law: laws that relate to relatives, laws that relate to disputes and reconciliation. All of that is addressed through the concept of *as-sulh*—how to rectify one's affair and to come back together when there is disharmony.

Verse number 36 is an interesting verse in this *surah*. It is near the beginning of this *juz*, and Allah (s.w.t.) gives ten commandments to you and I. Allah says, "*Worship Allah and associate nothing with Him.*" And then He says to take good care of your parents and to look after those who are very close relatives to you who the tie of the womb ties together, the orphans, those who are impoverished and poor (not necessarily to mean that they have nothing; they may have work but perhaps their ends do not meet), and your nearest neighbours, the one that is right next door to you. You were given instructions by Allah to look after these people: the community in general, those who surround you; your friend, the one who lives near you and whom you consider as your mate; the one who is travelling and is foreign to your land, the one who is a refugee, the one who is not from your area and territory, from your ethnicity, from your race; and whomever Allah has given to you to be in charge of—they are in your duty to look after and to care for. Allah says that these are essential rights that we will be questioned about on the Day of Judgement.

In verse 41, it is as if Allah is saying that these are the rights we have over each other, but the Prophet (s.a.w.) has a greater right above us. And Allah's right upon him was that he was to look after all of us, which was a heavy burden upon the Prophet (s.a.w.). There is a verse in the Qur'an that made the Prophet (s.a.w.) cry. In the famous hadith by Ibn Mas'ud (r.a.), it was narrated that the Prophet (s.a.w.) asked Ibn Mas'ud to recite the Qur'an. He began from Surah An-Nisa' until he reached verse 41. *What will be the condition on the Day of Judgement when we bring witness unto mankind from every nation and I bring you, o' Muhammad, as a witness above all humanity?* An enormous task and burden to carry.

Allah (s.w.t.) continues to speak about discovering the truth and of those who change the truth to suit their sinful desires. He also warns us about playing around with scriptures. Here, Allah begins to address the hypocrites, and one of the main special interest that this *surah* addresses are the conditions of hypocrisy, the attitude of the hypocrites, how they view themselves and how they should be viewed by others. One of the things that are important as to the signs of hypocrisy are those that relate to self-evidence, i.e., you are to worry and look at yourself first before you look out for hypocrisy in others.

Allah (s.w.t.) also speaks about looking at what other people have. Do not look and be critical of what Allah has given to some that perhaps you have been deprived of. This applies to all segments of interactions—amongst men, women, and neighbours towards each other. It is a major theme that is found in this *surah*.

Allah then begins to speak about *amanah* (trust). He gives an instruction that you *must* fulfil the trust towards those to whom the trust belongs. The fulfilment of trust is tied to the overarching theme of releasing oppression and of doing just by people, particularly the weakest. These include men who are weak in the physical and financial sense, orphans, women, the destitute, and the widowed. Allah speaks about this in clear terms, and

He invites those who have the concept of *amanah* to teach it and to instil it in others.

Allah then speaks about obedience to Him, to His Messenger, and to those who have been established as leaders amongst you. The Prophet (s.a.w.) taught us that leaders should be followed, even when they are not entirely the best of people, so long as they are not forbidding us from what is commanded by Allah. This revolutionary spirit, the *takfiri* and the *khariji*, is something condemnable in the Qur'an.

After that, Allah immediately begins to discuss the characters of the hypocrites. It is as if Allah is saying that those who do not give their religion to Allah and the Messenger and are rebellious against the leadership have the characteristics of hypocrisy. One of the characteristics of hypocrisy is that they do not stand up for prayer; when they do, they do not remember Allah often. They come to and perform the prayer sluggishly and lazily. The only reason they pray is that people see them from a vantage point. Their remembrance of God is little, and therefore Allah uses them as an example for you and me to be worried about. Increase your prayer, be vigilant in your *salah*, be vigilant in reading your Qur'an, and be accepting of the leadership of Allah and His Messenger and those who call us to that which is good.

Allah also warns us about signs of the hypocrite. These people are fluent in their recitation of the Qur'an, but they do not understand it. *Do they not ponder, understand, reflect and deeply analyse the Qur'an? And if it came from other than Allah, they would find dispute in it.*

Allah also asks us to be from those who take caution during times of warfare and hostility, which is something in the context of the revelation of this *surah*. It was experienced by Prophet Muhammad (s.a.w.), and the lesson to be taken here is that we should be careful and be on guard; otherwise, the enemy may slight against you in one push.

Allah speaks about the sinfulness of killing, harming other people, fighting amongst Muslims and killing another believer—all of these things are condemnable and specifically mentioned in this chapter.

Towards the end of this *juz*, Allah commands that even during times of warfare, we must be vigilant of our prayer. Perhaps we may assume that due to all this warfare, we can delay our prayer. No. Allah has actually legislated *salatul khauf*—the prayer during the time of fear. In these same verses, Allah also states that the prayer is written to be prayed at precise times. Not even during times of warfare can we delay it.

Finally, Allah ends this *juz* by again reflecting on the hypocrites—that they have their laziness, their inability to make their *dhikr*, their seek to produce dissension and rebellion amongst the ranks of believers, and their hearts that are not with Allah and His Messenger, Muhammad (s.a.w.). May Allah protect us from these. 🌼

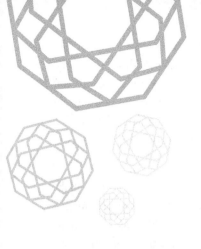

JUZ 6

Juz 6 begins at the end of Surah An-Nisa', the fourth chapter of the Qur'an. Allah (s.w.t.) begins by speaking about the innocence of Maryam (a.s.) against the false accusations that were being circulated of her. Similarly for 'Isa (a.s.) and the false accusation that was made about him, his alleged divinity, that he is the son of God, and how these and other similar types of false claims were put to rest.

Allah pays particular close attention to the claim that Jesus was crucified and to the theology of the cross. Jesus was not killed, he was not put on a cross, but it was made to seem so. Allah speaks of this in great detail and puts an end to the discussion according to our creed and theology as Muslims.

Allah then goes on to warn against those who take extremes in their religion. "*O people of the Book! Do not go to extremes regarding your faith.*" Do not hold on to particular theology that is not true. And that becomes a central point that Allah indirectly warns our community of Muslims about as well.

Allah then speaks about the prophets of Allah. These are all messengers of Allah. He gives an exhaustive list of many of the messengers that He has sent on to mankind, those whom we know and those of whom we have not heard of.

The *surah* then ends very much in the same way that it began, where Allah speaks about the oppression that is seen by some, and that the laws of inheritance are meant to ensure that women are given their share and entitlement into the blessings that may arrive upon the passing of one of their parents, spouses and so on, and that they are not to be overlooked and abused.

Surah Al-Ma'idah, which is the fifth chapter, begins with a very strong instruction from Allah, for us to be from those who maintain the contracts that we have promised. Surah Al-Ma'idah is also the last *surah* of the Qur'an that is revealed in relation to laws, rules, and regulations given to our *ummah* through the Prophet Muhammad (s.a.w.). Some of the stipulations, rules, and regulations discussed relate to contracts, regulations, family lives, divorce, ihram, pilgrimage, matters that relate to sacrifice, obligations that we have towards one another, to society, and even to those who form part of the society but who do not believe in what we believe—whether in our majority or in our minority in their land.

The very first verse begins with a command for us to maintain our contractual stipulations. This *surah* is also very unique; it has 18 *ahkam*—laws that are instituted which abrogate or are not abrogated by other verses in the Qur'an. For example, in the previous Surah An-Nisa', Allah declares, "*Do not approach prayer while you are intoxicated.*" Here, Allah definitively says you are not allowed to consume intoxicant. Within this *surah*, Allah has 18 rules and regulations that undo or repeal other rules that are found in other sections of the Qur'an. There is no ruling in this *surah* that is abrogated anywhere else in the Qur'an, because it is one of the last chapters revealed to the Prophet (s.a.w.).

It has in it the verses on to how to perform *wudu'*, how to make *ghusl*, and the rules which relate to them in the most generic sense. Allah also continues to speak about some of the injustices that occur, one of which is false testimony and the breaking of contractual stipulations. In the previous *surah*, Allah tells us to "*be persistently standing firm in justice, witnesses for Allah, even if it be against yourselves or parents and relatives*"—

even if it is against your family, or your loved ones. And this becomes a basic premise that justice is meant for all, inclusive of the believers. Disbelief, in turn, is shown as being critical to identify and to be kept distant from. Allah says, "*They have certainly disbelieved who say, 'Allah is the third of three*" or that Allah is divisible or that Jesus is the son of Allah. It is a very strict and strong statement.

The story of Qabil and Habil (Cain and Abel) is also discussed in Surah Al-Ma'idah. Allah discusses the details of that first murder committed, and the Prophet (s.a.w.) would later say, "*Whenever a person is murdered unjustly, there is a share from the burden of the crime on the first son of Adam for he was the first to start the tradition of murdering.*"

Allah then speaks about the trials of Musa (a.s.), not just with Fir'awn but also with Bani Isra'il. Musa came to his people and said to them, "*O my people, enter the Holy Land...*" to indicate to them that they have to struggle for it, fight for it, and give their lives for it, if need be. Instead, their reply was, "*O' Musa, indeed we will not enter it, ever, as long as they are within it; so go, you and your Lord, and fight. Indeed, we are remaining right here.*" It is also an indirect way of Allah giving support to the *sahabah* who said that they would not say to the Prophet (s.a.w.) what the people of Musa said to him. Rather, they would say, *We will come with you and we will strive for that which is right, o' Messenger of Allah.*

Allah continues by speaking about the importance of charity and putting one's trust in Allah—that it is not just about your numbers, your power, your authority, your strength, or your economic prowess. Rather, it is about one's faithfulness to Allah. And when there are times of stress and difficulty, this is the time that Allah is preparing us for greater things in life.

Allah then speaks about the sanctity of life. He orders us to be from those who are very careful with the rights and responsibilities that we give to one another. Allah says that for the one who gives life—who saves a life—it is as if he has given life to all of humanity, and for the one who brings death to a soul that has not been legislated, it is as if he has brought destruction upon all of humanity. May Allah save us from that.

Allah also warns us about the evil of corruption. Do not destroy the earth and cause corruption in it, do not murder, do not destroy the environment and everything that surrounds us. Be from those who are balanced in that regard.

Allah then continues to speak about the importance of revelation, and that revelation is the guiding force that Allah has sent for us in humanity, and to follow its governance. Allah says that the ones who do not follow governance and rule, nor appreciate the power of what has been given in His revelation to guide humanity to that which is right, are from those who have disbelieved, who have rebelled and deviated from the path of honour and truth. Therefore, as Muslims, we sanctify the importance of the Qur'an and the tradition of the Prophet (s.a.w.) in our lives.

Allah also speaks about allying or joining in partnership with others against the believers. This was a very contemporary issue during the life of the Prophet (s.a.w.), where they were warned against making such alliances that would exclude other believers in that way.

The *juz* ends with Allah introducing 'Isa (a.s.) and the struggles that he would endure, including the false claims that were made against him. 'Isa (a.s.) was a man, a prophet, and a sign to humanity. He was the word of God—"*Be,*" and he was created. All of that shows that 'Isa (a.s.) was not divine, and every miracle that Allah mentions about 'Isa (a.s.) was something that was performed by other prophets as a miracle bestowed on to them by Allah. This becomes clear in the opening of Juz 7. ❀

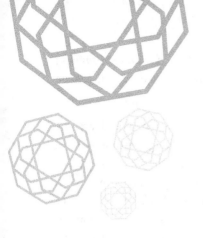

Juz 7 is at the end of Surah Al-Ma'idah, the fifth chapter of the Qur'an. Allah (s.w.t.) initially speaks about those who are distinct and have a quarrel with the Muslims, particularly at the time of the Prophet (s.a.w.). Some of them were from the Jewish tribes who lived around the Prophet, and some were those near to him in affection and affinity—in particular, some of the Christian monks and so forth. When they turned to the scripture and they heard of the Qur'an, it was something that brought faith into their hearts, and they could find the similarity between them.

In this *surah*, Allah moves quickly to speak about some elements of the *fiqh*, rules and regulations that are found in this chapter. Some of the unique aspects of *fiqh* are, for example, how one would expiate a vow or *qasm*.

For instance, if you have said, *My God, I will do this,* and you were not able to do it, how then would you expiate it.

Further elements of *fiqh* that were raised are the prohibition of intoxicants, gambling, astrology and believing that the movement of the stars somehow influences day-to-day life, hunting when one is in the state of ihram, and so on. Allah also speaks about the *wasiyyah*, our final will and testament. Becoming a witness and the conditions of how to witness the contracts of others are also addressed, and mention is also made of the fact that witnessing contracts is a noble pursuit. Allah also tells us how to write a contract when there are no witnesses who we are able to rely on. All of those are *fiqh* matters that are found in this chapter.

Then Allah begins to look once again at 'Isa (a.s.). He was introduced in the early part of this *juz* and in the last part of the last *juz*. 'Isa (a.s.) and his disciples are brought into focus where they are having a conversation. Allah says, *Recount on to them on the blessings that I am giving you, o' 'Isa, that I have allowed you to bring the dead to life by My power, to create bird out of mud and clay by My power, to cure the blind and hear the deaf by My power. O' 'Isa, mention that to them.* And yet, after having experienced all this, they said, *We want one more. We want you to bring down a table spread* (Al-Ma'idah, from where this chapter gets its name)*, food from heaven* *that we can consume and eat.* Allah said, *I will bring it down for you, and for the one who disbelieves thereafter, I will punish them in a way that none will be punished after them.* May Allah protect us from this punishment. Once again, it is Allah's indirect way of honouring the *sahabah* of the Prophet (s.a.w.). Initially, in the last *juz*, there were honoured because they went and struggled along with the Prophet (s.a.w.), unlike the Israelites. And here once again, they did not question the Prophet (s.a.w.) about his nobility and prophethood to a degree that was an agitation, as was the case with 'Isa (a.s.) and his disciples.

The *surah* comes to an end when Allah then speaks to 'Isa (a.s.) in a future tense. *Did you ask these people to worship you instead of Me? Did you ask them to take your mother as a deity that they would make Hail Marys as her name?* 'Isa says, *How can I say what I have no right to say? If I have ever said something like this, You would already know, o' Allah. I only said "Worship Allah—my Lord and your Lord".* 'Isa (a.s.) then continues, *O' Allah, if you wish to punish them, they are nothing more than your servants, but if you forgive them, then you are The Forgiving.* May Allah give us His forgiveness.

Chapter 6, Surah Al-An'am (The Cattle), which forms part of Juz 7, begins now, affirming Allah's singular unity of power. It is almost as if the end of Surah Al-Ma'idah enters into Surah Al-An'am as a segue. Allah begins Surah Al-An'am by saying "*Alhamdulillah,*" and all of Surah Al-An'am is actually about the splendour in the power of Allah (s.w.t.). In fact, all of the stories that are mentioned in it are related to that.

The *surah* begins with the praise of Allah as a testament to His oneness and His unity of power. At the end of the *surah*, we recite, "*Indeed, my prayer, my rites of sacrifice, my living and my dying are for Allah, Lord of the worlds.*" Therefore, this *surah* seeks to establish the supremacy of Allah. Once again, this *surah* is one of the long chapters of the Qur'an.

In this *surah*, Allah admonishes those who turn away from Him. Ibrahim (a.s.) is given as an example of the one who turned away from those who worshipped other than Allah and then began to discover Allah. Allah gives insight into the fact that a person can come to strengthen their faith in Allah by seeing and observing that which is around him. Ibrahim (a.s.) is given as a pillar of *tawhid*. He looked into the heavens and questioned, and he asked Allah in his prayer, "*If my Lord does not guide me, I shall be one of those who go astray.*" He became a person who was awake with faith. He questioned his father, he questioned his people, and he bounced from one community to another, persecuted on account of his faith. It is as if the Prophet (s.a.w.) was being met with this example that would happen to him in time.

Involved in all of these are nations that were destroyed. They were given as examples to the Prophet (s.a.w.) and his people. *If you do not adjust yourself and if you do not come to faith, then just as the nations that had been destroyed before you, your nation and your people can be destroyed.* All of these are signs that revelation is something that can be paralleled to the physical, observable world that can strengthen your belief in that which has been revealed to us by Allah. Therefore, science and intellectualism are never at odds with Islam. We are not of those who say, *Do not study science because you can only study the Qur'an.* Rather we are drawn to always see the things that are compatible. This is the example that we see in Surah Al-An'am.

Allah then begins to speak about His majesty. *It is Allah who breaks apart this seed, and plants it, and allows it to fruit. Who other than Allah can bring life from death and death out of life?* It is as if Allah is saying to look around, take inspiration from this universe, and have *tafakkur* and *tadabbur*—ponder about it, think and use your rationale—and you will be pointed to the fact that everything that did not exist could not have come into the existence without the influence of The Innovator of the heavens and the earth. You will find this statement of Allah in Surah Al-An'am.

At the end of this *juz*, Allah speaks about the spread of the cattle and the spread of the animals, and this is one of the places where this *surah* gets its name. It is a powerful *juz* of the Qur'an that speaks of the beauty and the majesty of Allah's power and the intricacy of His assistance to us in life. ⬡

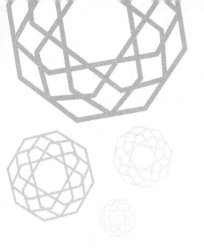

JUZ 8

Allah begins Juz 8, which nears the end of Surah Al-An'am, by speaking about some of the *fiqh* regulations that are intertwined with issues of *aqidah* (faith) and faithfulness. Allah (s.w.t.) speaks about animals that are killed or slaughtered without the name of Allah being mentioned on them, whether we should consume them or not. Allah also speaks about what is *halal* and *haram* for us, and on the impermissibility to consume the meat of slaughtered animals that have been made as offerings for false deities or gods, or at non-Islamic rituals of worship.

Allah transitions to speak about *al-hidayah* (guidance) and makes it known that guidance only comes from Him. It is not on account of our own doing that we discover guidance. When guidance comes, the chest of a person is opened for them to see the truth, their heart is exposed to the truth, and they are willing to accept it, because within their heart was the capacity to recognise the truth that is known to Allah, and so Allah led them to it. Therefore, faith is made equal to life; whereas *shirk*—disobedience to Allah, polytheism, and worshipping other false deities—is made equal to spiritual death.

Allah also speaks about the false deviations of *shaytan* when a person offers himself in worship to other than Allah (s.w.t.) or when a person prays to other than Allah. These are things that will lead a person further and further away from the straight path.

Then, Allah speaks in two verses about the great ten commandments. Allah (s.w.t.) says, *O' Muhammad, tell them our ten sacred things that Allah has commanded upon you.* That you do not worship other than Allah; that you be good to your parents; that you do not kill a child on account of being in poverty or disgrace; that the open and private sins that are vulgar and audacious (including sexual immorality, adultery, and things that are condemnable by all in society); that you do not murder; that you do not consume the wealth of orphans; that you do not cheat people in matters of business (do not wrongfully or deceitfully weigh things and be very careful in one's ethics); that you be upright in your truthfulness; and that keep any promises you make in God's name; and that this is the straight path of Allah—a path of life—so follow it and do not follow other ways.

In verse 162, Allah tells us, "*Say, 'Indeed, my prayer, my rites of sacrifice, my living and my dying are for Allah, Lord of the worlds.'*" The *surah* comes to an end with that admonition.

Allah then begins the seventh chapter of the Qur'an, Surah Al-A'raf. It can be translated as the heights that lead to Jannah or the trespassers up in the elevations. This is a *surah* that begins with four letters: *Alif Lam Mim Sad*. Allah begins this *surah* by condemning *shaytan*, to show us the mindset of *shaytan*, so that we can be aware of the '*shaytanic*' mode of thought. *I am better than him. I am of this genius. I am better than this Adam that You have created, I have always been good, but why have You preferred him to me? When I have been commanded, I have the choice to not fulfil the command of my Lord.* Therefore, Allah (s.w.t.) shows us this established mindset, so that we can be aware of it and stay distant from it.

Then Allah (s.w.t.) uncovers for us the enmity that *shaytan* has towards us human beings, especially as to how it began with Adam (a.s.). *Shaytan* wanted to remove the honour of Adam (a.s.), expose to him his humanness, to show him his privacy. This is a way of saying to Adam (a.s.), *You are just a mortal being*; although what *shaytan* was offering him, *If you eat from that tree—if you disobey the order of Allah—you will be from these angels, and you will live forever in happiness.* Allah shows to us that *shaytan* seeks to use our own desire (Adam [a.s.] desired the tree) and inflate it. Within us, we have the *nafs* and *hawwa* (desire), and *shaytan* capitalises on it by pushing us and tipping us over with his whispers. It is not he who commits the act—it is you who do it, by listening to those incantations and inspirations from *shaytan*.

Finally, Allah mentions that the *shaytan* is a silent whisperer who does not take the blame for our fault. And that *shaytan*—may Allah (s.w.t.) keep us protected from him—will come to us from all angles: from the front, from behind, from the right, and from the left. His aim is to prove and to show Allah that we will not be thankful and have *shukr* to Allah (s.w.t.). Therefore, one of the greatest ways that you subdue *shaytan* in your life is that you are from those who are thankful.

Allah then speaks about Adam (a.s.) and speaks *to* Adam (a.s.) and his children, which is us. *O' children of Adam (a.s.), do not let shaytan test you and meddle with you as he tested your parents before you and extracted them from Jannah and removed from them their garments. The garments of piety, that is what is best.* Meaning, you should surround yourself with piety and have righteousness in your conduct and your attire.

I want to highlight verse 33 in Surah Al-A'raf, because the *'ulama* have said that in this one verse are all the categories of what constitutes *haram*. Allah has prohibited for you all open acts of vulgar sin, whether you try to hide it, whether it is private or open, whether it is sexual immorality or intoxication—all of those; and to delay doing acts of obedience or to neglect doing that which is good. It is not just about doing wrong but it is also about not doing the right thing that you should do. That includes things like not fasting, not praying, not giving *zakah*, and not going to *hajj* when you should. Allah speaks about the forms of oppression that are inward: that you have anger towards others or that you oppress them with your thoughts, with your jealousy, through your words, or through your actions and dealings. Finally, do not be from those who worship and take a share that should only be for Allah and divide it among others. Do not give from that which should only be for Allah, towards others—in devotion, in adoration, in love, in fear, and so on. Finally, do not speak about Allah in a way that you do not know, or speak about faith, belief, right and wrong, *halal* and *haram*, without the surety of knowledge—this is one of the gravest sins. This verse therefore encapsulates all of the sinful things that a person may fall into.

Then Allah transitions into speaking about a debate between the people of heaven and the people of hell. When the people of heaven enter Jannah, they say to the people of hell, *Have you found what the promise of Allah was? That if you were to be sinful, you would be punished?*

Because we have found His promise to be true, that we had done righteousness, and Allah has blessed us with this Jannah.

Finally, to end the chapter, Allah speaks about five prophets who are given as examples to Prophet Muhammad (s.a.w.): Hud (a.s.) who was sent to the people of 'Ad, Saleh (a.s.) who was sent to the people of Thamud, Lut (a.s.) who was to the people of Sodom and Gomorrah, Shu'ayb (a.s.) who was sent to the people of Madyan, and finally Musa (a.s.) who was sent to Fir'awn and Bani Isra'il. Musa (a.s.) comes in at the beginning of the next *juz*. Allah speaks about the four as a prelude to Musa (a.s.). All of them began by saying, "*O my people! Worship Allah—you have no other god except Him.*" But all of them are mocked, jeered, and treated with oppression. Therefore, it is as if Allah is saying to the Prophet (s.a.w.), *Be ready, this is what happened before, and you need to be ready for it.* And the final example of Musa (a.s.) comes in the next *juz*. 🔶

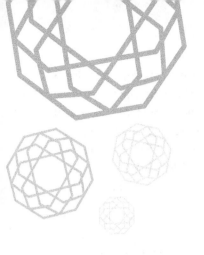

Juz 9 begins with some introductory pages of Surah Al-A'raf. Allah has just spoken about four of His prophets, and now he adds a fifth, Musa (a.s.). Initially, when they came to bring their message, all of the messengers and prophets were rejected and ostracised by their people. Allah (s.w.t.) says, *No messengers were sent to the people and the people rejected them, except that I sent upon them the severity of punishment, and that people who were punished before your people, o' Muhammad, experienced that. But your nation is salvaged because of your presence, as you are rahmatan lil 'alamin—a mercy to mankind.*

Allah (s.w.t.) then speaks immediately about the story of Musa (a.s.) with Fir'awn. There is no interlude that firstly discusses Musa's upbringing, that he was thrown in a river by his mother in a basket—none of that. It immediately enters with *"Then We sent after them Musa with Our signs to Fir'awn and his establishment."*

When Musa (a.s.) confronted Fir'awn, the latter challenged Musa by saying "Show us signs." And so this was when Musa (a.s.) demonstrated the signs that were given to him by Allah (s.w.t.). Fir'awn's magicians interjected, and they submitted to Allah by declaring, "*We have believed in the Lord of the worlds—the Lord of Musa and Harun,*" and they became among the faithful.

Allah (s.w.t.) then shows us that Musa (a.s.) continued to invite the people—those who believed in him—to remain patient upon faith when he said to them, *Hold on to prayers and hold on to your faithfulness, it will increase you in patience.*

Allah then begins to speak about the incident after they were saved and Fir'awn and his army were destroyed. Musa (a.s.) left initially for thirty days and did not return until forty nights after. Allah (s.w.t.) says, "*And We made an appointment with Musa for thirty nights and perfected them by [the addition of] ten.*" During this time, Musa (a.s.) was given the Tablet—the ten sacred commandments by Allah. But at that moment, the people of Musa could not maintain their faithfulness. When he returned to his people, he saw that they were worshipping a false god—a golden calf. Musa (a.s.) was so angered by this that he put down the Tablet. *My people are not ready for this.* After that, the curse of Allah (s.w.t.) descended upon them, until Musa (a.s.) asked Allah for forgiveness on behalf of himself and his people, and

Allah accepted their repentance. Musa (a.s.) is now put into trial, not by Fir'awn but by his own people. When he invited them to do good, they were quarrelsome and rebellious, and it took forty years for that to be purged from them. They had to be broken by the earth and by the travel until they could completely submit themselves to Allah (s.w.t.).

Allah then mentions the story of those who broke the covenant of the Sabbath. The Jewish people were prohibited from doing any work on the Sabbath, but they thought they could trick Allah. They would put their fishing nets out the night before so that the nets could trap the fish, even though they were not supposed to earn or do anything; they were supposed to trust that Allah will provide their food for them. So the fish would come into the nets, and they would pull the nets out on Sunday. It is as if they were trying to play with the scripture of Allah (s.w.t.).

This *surah* is very powerful. It has the story of Musa (a.s.), and it is meant to say to the Prophet (s.a.w.), *The trials that came before you are very similar to the trials you will face.* This *surah* also speaks to the Jewish people who were living in Madinah, *You recognise the truth of Muhammad. You recognise that he has come with sure signs and spirit which calls to that which is similar to Musa, and that which preceded him. You recognise that this is a form of truth, and you do not deny him for any reason other than for hostility, pride and anger, hoping that your final messenger would have been from your own ethnicity. But because he has come from a different group, from the tribe of Isma'il rather than the tribe of Ishaq.* So Allah speaks about this in very clear ways.

The *surah* comes to an end with a *sajdah* to Allah in the very last verse. This *sajdah* to Allah in the last verse of the *surah* is unique to this *surah*, so if you are praying behind your *imam* in *taraweeh*, you will do a *sajdah* in it.

Allah then begins Surah Al-Anfal, which is the *surah* that details the Battle of Badr: what preceded it, the emotions of the *sahabah*, their overwhelming sense of fear and foreboding and how Allah calmed them, how Allah let them slumber and washed them with a cleansing rain. Allah reassured them, saying, *Is it not enough that you are given a thousand angels to come and defend you?*

The opening verses of this chapter are very important. They asked the Prophet (s.a.w.) about the spoils of war. They went out for the Battle of Badr, full of hope, and now that they had won, they asked, *What do we do with all of these spoils? Never in our wildest dreams did we think we would be this victorious.* Allah says, "*Their distribution is decided by Allah and His Messenger.*" Allah will determine it through His Messenger, Muhammad (s.a.w.).

Then Allah speaks about the key to victory in life. Have *taqwAllah*; put the fear, the consciousness, the awareness, the love, and the hope you have in Allah as the centre of your life. And rectify your affairs between each other; do not let there be any enmity between you and your brothers or your sisters, and remove any pride, hate, or racism from your heart—come together. Obey Allah and His Messenger if you are truly believers. Those three ingredients brought together will give a person a level of victory in everything that they face in life. Allah then adds of it. The believers are those who, when Allah's name is mentioned or His revelations are the recited, their hearts are in awe and shudder of it, and it is something that calms them and gives them deliverance and strength in Allah (s.w.t.). When His name is mentioned, it gives them the ability to trust Allah and to go further than they thought they could go. The sign that you have faith in your heart and trust in Allah is that you maintain your prayers and you give in charity, not withholding it for yourself.

Allah then tells about the angels descending in the Battle of Badr, how victory was given to the believers and how He made the numbers of the believers seem small in the sight of the unbelievers. Allah (s.w.t.) says, *Fear Allah and do not fear anyone other than Him. He is the refuge of those who are fearful and He is The One who when you are surrounded, opens for you an exit.*

Allah ends this *juz* in the very last closing verses by saying that those who disbelieve will expend great vast amounts of wealth to try and distract and deter people from the path of God. They will give their wealth, but it will be something that becomes a sorrow upon them, and they eventually will be brought to destruction and loss because of it. So do not be sad. The amount of resources that are given to those who oppose you, eventually they will spend it—you cannot stop it. You will be given ascendancy and victory. This is where this *juz* closes.

JUZ *10*

In this *juz*, Allah (s.w.t.) continues speaking about the Battle of Badr. This battle was intentional—it was to bring peace to the believers, who were always worried as to what they would do when the enemy came to attack. It also brought to bear the punishment that the people of Quraysh would eventually see, and that began at the Battle of Badr. Their chiefs 'Uqbah, Abu Jahl, and 'Utbah were all killed on that day. It was a demoralising defeat for them, even more so spiritually.

The *surah* then speaks about how to gain Allah's assistance. Allah (s.w.t.) says, *"When you encounter a company (from the enemy forces), stand firm and remember Allah much that you may be successful. And obey Allah and His Messenger, and do not dispute and (thus) lose courage and (then) your strength would depart; and be patient."*

Hold on to each other and be firm with each other. If you do not do this, your energy, efficiency, and strength will depart. There will be things in which you have to be patient.

In disputes we have with people whom we are supposed to see eye to eye with, we have to be patient. Do not be like those who leave their homes for a noble purpose, but then ruin it because of pride, arrogance, showing-off, and boastfulness. None of that will be pleasing to Allah (s.w.t.). In the end, what is taught is to obey Allah, His Messenger (s.a.w.), and to be brothers to each other.

This is how Surah Al-Anfal comes to an end.

The ninth chapter of the Qur'an is Surah At-Tawbah. This is a chapter where there is agreement among the scholars that the *basmalah* (*bismillahir-rahmanir-rahim*) should not be recited. The *surah* descended to affirm Allah's wrath and anger against those who renegaded against the Prophet (s.a.w.), from the people of Quraysh to the Arabs who did not believe, and more importantly, from the hypocrites who lived with disbelief in their hearts but showed an aspect of faithfulness on the outside.

The *surah* has different names; another is Bara'ah, which means disavowal. There is no mention of mercy at the beginning of the *surah*; instead, it begins by discussing the peace treaty that the Prophet had with the people of Quraysh. The condition of the treaty was that it would be honoured up to the date that was set, and thereafter there would be no more treaty. Therefore, it would be something where the Prophet (s.a.w.) would take action. This is where the practice of idolatry in the realm of the holy sanctuaries of Makkah, Madinah, and so forth was brought to an end. After that year, the idolators were prohibited from entering into the holy sites to do their idolatrous act of worship. That was the commandment set by Allah (s.w.t.).

Allah speaks often in this *surah* about the *masajid* (mosques). There is one mosque called Dirar that will be mentioned in the next *juz* for being a mosque that was ill-intentioned. But in this *juz*, Allah speaks about the mosque that honours Allah—a place where His name is mentioned and praised. Hypocrites have an allergic reaction to this. They are dishonoured because they do not have love and affinity for the house of Allah.

Allah also mentions that there are twelve months of the calendar year, and four of which are to be treated as sacred, where violence, war and sin should be abstained from in even particular regard. There is also a virtue that is set for the early *muhajirin*, those who made *hijrah* to Madinah. They cannot be made equal to those who stayed behind, and even the *ansar* who received the *muhajirin* are not on equal standing with them.

Allah also speaks about defending the believers, and that there are a call and a time to bear arms. In Surah Al-Anfal and Surah At-Tawbah, the Prophet (s.a.w.) is told, *Raise an army and raise strength, and deter violence against you by positioning yourself strategically in a strengthening pose*. The believers who have faith in Allah are those who struggle in the path of truth, commit the *jihad* that Allah requests of their life and their wealth to stand up for a greater purpose and to defend those who are the weakest among them. Allah has bestowed nobility upon those who are martyred in the cause of defending others in their path of truth. Those who give their life, energy, and wealth for the service of others are those who are the most noble of people.

Allah also continues by speaking about the categories of *zakah*. There is a lot of financial discussion in this *surah* where Allah speaks about *zakah*, which is distinguished from general charity. Allah separates the two. For general charity, you decide how much you give, whom you give it to, when you give—it is up to you. But *zakah* is to be paid to certain categories and types of people listed in verse 60. There is no choice in this. It is determined by the calculation set by Allah (s.w.t.).

Allah also speaks about the hypocrites wanting to hoard their wealth. Their wealth that they hoard will be a source of punishment for them on the Day of Judgement. They will be asked to bear its burden.

Hypocrites are those who are harmful to others, unethical in their business dealings, and forget the share of the needy and the poor. They are compared to those who are righteous, who give freely in the path of Allah; in turn, Allah returns it to them often. Allah then compares the hypocrites at the time of the Prophet (s.a.w.) to those nations that were perished and destroyed in the past, especially those who had clergy greedy and coveted wealth and money.

The great underlying theme of this *surah* is that there are hypocrites amongst the believers, and that hypocrites are those who will not stand up for truth nor bear arms to defend it and will not hold the Prophet (s.a.w.) in esteem and awe. Although they will stand behind him in prayer, in their hearts there are suspicion, malice, and anger. They were trying to profiteer from this to make wealth. They belittle the believers at every turn, and they look down at the contributions that the believers give. Allah juxtaposes that to those who are true in faith: they are those who are courageous and giving, and even when they do not have enough, they give and spend what they have generously in the path of Allah, what is beyond even their means at times. These two grooves were always found within the *ummah* of the Prophet Muhammad (s.a.w.).

JUZ 11

This is near the middle and the end of Surah At-Tawbah, which is a chapter in the Qur'an where we do not recite the *basmalah* at the beginning of the *surah*. It is a *surah* that has three important purposes. But the most important theme here is that Allah will suffice for the Prophet (s.a.w.) and his *ummah*.

There are instructions initially on how to deal with those who are brought to the Prophet (s.a.w.) and do not believe in him: those who are contesting him in warfare, who have broken peace treaties with him, and who have committed certain things that have brought about agitation for the Prophet. The second is on how to deal with those who are living amongst the believers as hypocrites: those who do not believe in God nor believe in the Prophet (s.a.w.), but are pretending and seeking for a moment of weakness so that they can pounce on him. And in the third, it speaks about those who value the Messenger of Allah: the *sahabah*, the *muhajirin*, and the *ansar*.

This *juz* begins where Allah (s.w.t.) classifies and distinguishes the people who were living in Madinah: they were the *muhajirin*, the elite, and then under them, the *ansar*. Allah (s.w.t.) says, "*And the first forerunners [in the faith] among the muhajirin and the ansar...*" If you put this verse with other verses in the Qur'an, for example in Surah Al-Waqi'ah where Allah classifies the believers on the Day of Judgement, He uses the same words. Therefore, Allah is referring to a very select group of people—they are those who have given and struggled for the path of Allah and in defence of the Prophet (s.a.w.). May Allah make us one of them and reach their level.

Then Allah speaks about Al-A'rab. In the surrounding tribes of the Arabs, there were the Bedouins. Some of them were very strong in their *kufr* and their hate of truth and monotheism. There were also others whom Allah speaks about in praiseworthy terms. And then there were the hypocrites, who were found in and around Madinah society. There were more than 70 of them grouped together, and they would mock the Prophet (s.a.w.) in their privacy. Allah would relate to the Prophet what was said, and he would confront some of them. They would reply, *We were just joking around and we were just making jest. We were not serious in our condemnation of you, o' Muhammad.*

Another transition point is where Allah speaks about Masjid Dirar. The hypocrites tried to set up a mosque that rivalled the first mosque built by the Prophet (s.a.w.), Masjid Quba', which was built on the foundation of piety. *A note here, that for the one who visits Quba' and makes wudu in their home before attending to it, they will get the magnificent reward of an 'umrah.*

Although Masjid Dirar was a mosque dedicated to the worship of Allah, the intention behind it was false. Allah (s.w.t.) says, *Do not ever stand in prayer in it, o' Muhammad, even though they invited you, there is a prohibition to pray in it.* This teaches us a very important element and principle in our faith: actions are judged and are implemented on account of their intentions. So we do not look at the building and infrastructure, but what it is raised for and what are the intentions behind it.

Allah then speaks about the believers from whom He has purchased their lives and their wealth—how they struggled in the path of Allah (s.w.t.). He also speaks about those who died in a state of hypocrisy. When 'Abdullah ibn 'Ubayy ibn Salul died, his righteous son came to the Prophet (s.a.w.) and said, *My father has died, please make du'a for him.* The Prophet stood at his grave and made *du'a,* and Allah forbade him. *Do not stand at his grave and do not make du'a for him.* Because they were disbelievers. From here, we can see Allah's ruling for a person who has died in an agitated state of unbelief and disbelief in Allah—they are unworthy of prayers and mercy from the believers—and that is something settled in the Qur'an.

Then Allah (s.w.t.) talks about *tawbah* (repentance). Here, it is about the *tawbah* of the three men who had missed the Battle of Tabuk. This battle took place in a season where the fruit had ripened and the shade had become pleasant. There were so many hypocrites who made excuses for not attending the battle, but among them are these three righteous believers, the most prominent of them being Ka'ab (r.a.). They regretted themselves and told the Prophet (s.a.w.) the truth. However, Allah was very decisive in His words thereafter, and they were ostracised from the community. No one spoke to them, not even their wives would say *Assalamualaikum* to them. They were cut off until their repentance to Allah was proven and they had done what was worthy of their repentance. The element of this chapter—Surah At-Tawbah—can be seen from this.

The closing verses of this *juz* then are about attaching ourselves to the book of Allah. The merits of the *sahabah,* the first ones to come to faith, who felt the weakness of others, who took on the burden of carrying faith to us—we are only Muslims on account of them conveying it from the Prophet (s.a.w.). The closing verses of Surah At-Tawbah is a commendation of the love of the Prophet (s.a.w.) for his *ummah* and the love of the *ummah*, those who value him, back for him (s.a.w.).

This brings us into Surah Yunus. Surah Yunus is a majestic *surah* in honour of Allah (s.w.t.). Basically, the theme of Surah Yunus is that *you are going to be given many revelations, and a lot of them are going to require patience, and you need to look to those who came before you for inspiration, o' Muhammad and the ummah of Muhammad.*

Surah Yunus is very 'science-rich'—it contains many verses about the creation of the heavens and the earth. The three main sections of the *surah* are about *tawhid* (monotheism), the science and creations of Allah, and the reward of belief, the punishment of disbelief, and the mercy of Allah. In another section, Allah speaks about the attitude of those who oppose the first group. They will be from those on whom affliction will befall them. Allah will turn away from them, and His punishment will eventually reach them. They ask for miracles, they ask for a new Qur'an to descend upon them, and they ask about what makes Prophet Muhammad worthy of prophethood. They ask about what is going to come in the next life, and Allah gives the parable of this life in comparison to the hereafter.

They are told about Jannah. Allah speaks about Jannah to inspire the believers and also to show the disbelievers that there is something that they can aspire to. That the worldly life is a place where you try to earn your way with Allah (s.w.t.). That Allah is real, and we can find Allah's evidence in the creations that surround us.

Allah debates with the disbelievers and gives them numerous examples and signs that the Qur'an is full of advice and mercy. In it is a cure to that which ails the heart, and in it is a source of guidance.

Allah also speaks about *awliya'ullah*—those who befriended Allah and Allah, in turn, befriended them. They are those who have no sorrow nor fear. They do not feel them because they trust Allah, and in the next life, they will be assured of His magnificence and happiness. They are those who believe and who work righteous deeds through piety.

The final section of Surah Yunus brings an end to this *juz*, where Allah makes reference to previous prophets as practical examples for the Prophet (s.a.w.). Allah gives the example of Nuh (a.s.), Musa (a.s.), and Harun (a.s.). Allah also speaks about Yunus (a.s.), which is where the chapter gets its name. *Do not be like Yunus who left his people, and he was frustrated that they would not come to faith. So We tested him and then when We* returned him to them, We showed him that even without him, they came to belief. Meaning, o' Muhammad, you are a tool for Me to use in calling people to good and if I wish to remove you, I can still bring people to accept faith. 🌸

JUZ 12

The beginning of Juz 12 is on the second page of Surah Hud. The beginning verse is a magnificent one, which somewhat sets the theme for the *surah*, that Allah (s.w.t.) is Omnipotent. In verse 6, He says, "*And there is no creature on earth but that upon Allah is its provision.*" In this *surah*, Allah speaks about His grandeur, His majesty, who He is, and what He has provided for us as human beings and for everything that exists on this beautiful earth He has created for us. There are three essential themes in this *surah*: His majesty, the vastness of His knowledge, and Him being The Provider.

Allah also makes reference to the Qur'an as being a miracle that is sent by Him to humanity. In other places in the Qur'an, Allah says, *Bring something similar to it. If you cannot, then bring ten surahs similar to it. If you cannot, just bring one surah*. And they cannot. At the time of the Prophet (s.a.w.), they were at the height of Arabic culture and poetry. Nothing could be brought to rival the Qur'an. Therefore, the *surah* is set as something that talks about the *da'wah*, the preaching of the *deen*, and using the resources that Allah has provided us.

The first resource is the book of Allah. The Prophet (s.a.w.) had once said that Surah Hud and its sister surahs made his hair turn grey. Because it is something that shows the obligation of being a person who will be accountable to Allah (s.w.t.). So Allah establishes the book, and Allah speaks about the job of the one who preaches it.

Then Allah speaks about examples of the past. In essence, Allah (s.w.t.) gives the Prophet (s.a.w.) a crash training course and a technical framework. He speaks about so many prophets in this *surah*—Nuh (a.s.), Hud (a.s.), Saleh (a.s.), Ibrahim (a.s.), Lut (a.s.), Shu'ayb Shu'ayb, Musa (a.s.)—all of them are named in this one chapter and many of them with great detail.

The first prophet that is addressed in great detail is Nuh (a.s.). Allah speaks about the relationship between Nuh and his rebellious people. Then Allah identifies some of those rebellious people as being persons from his own family—his own wife and son, both of whom disbelieved in him and began to fulfil and deal wickedness in the land. Allah sees Nuh (a.s.) through the storm, and then Nuh witnessed his son drown in front of him, after inviting him to believe and climb into the ship of salvation. His son said, *Rather my father, I will climb up the mountain.* Nuh replied, *No one will protect you except Allah.* From here we learn that our love for Allah must transcend our love of anything and anyone else, even our beloved children.

Hud (a.s.) is a central figure, and this is where the *surah* gets its name. The greatest story mentioned of him is about the power of *istighfar*, asking for forgiveness. Hud was constantly inviting his people to turn back to Allah and ask for forgiveness. Allah then shows through this example that if we always made *istighfar* to Allah, there are two gains that can be obtained: a material, physical blessing in one's life where you will be given material wealth, happiness, and success; and an increase of your spiritual contentment and position with Allah on the Day of Judgement. It only strengthens you to humble yourself to Allah.

Allah also speaks about Hud (a.s.) and other prophets in terms of their patience and *tawakkul* (trusting Allah). It is an implicit way to say to the Prophet (s.a.w.), *I am going to shake the feet beneath you, o' Muhammad. Be patient, as others who came before you were required to be patient.*

When reference was made to Shu'ayb (a.s.), it shows Islam's care for financial responsibility and fiscal management, and that we should not be causing corruption in the land nor treating people with inequity.

Allah (s.w.t.) also gives the example during the time of Lut (a.s.)—of sexual immorality and the conduct and sexual cravings of people that step out of and go beyond biological norms, which are sinful within Islam.

Allah then gave the example of Ibrahim (a.s.) as being a tempered prophet, who had goodwill and hope even though he was rejected by every group of people that he encountered.

Finally, Allah speaks about His power to subjugate someone as tyrannical as Fir'awn.

In the last section of the *surah*, Allah speaks about connecting to Him. Allah (s.w.t.) says that if you establish your prayer, you remain steadfast, and you are a person of patience and perseverance with full trust in Allah, then you will be from those who find true happiness and contentment in life and in Jannah.

This *juz* then transitions into chapter 12, which is Surah Yusuf. Allah refers to this *surah* as the best of narrative stories that can be told, from which lessons can be extracted. This story is about Yusuf being tested in life, and that if you are patient when you are tested, then you will be blessed. It is also about humiliation; if you are tested with it and you remain patient and true, then you can be brought back to honour—from enslavement to kingship and being an authority in the land, from division and separation from your family to being brought and made whole and united again, from the grief of Ya'qub (a.s.) at the loss of not one but two of his sons and the treachery of his elder sons to the joy of reconciling and having peace, at hardships transitioning into ease so that the ease washes away the feeling of hardship, and from denial to the affirmation and acceptance of one's errors and sins of the past so as to free oneself through repentance. This story is also about love—the love of a father to his son, the love of material wealth, the love of attention—all of these are different kinds of righteous love and immoral love. The love of an infatuated woman, the love of sin—all of these are addressed in this *surah*.

Surah Yusuf is broken down into three important parts: the childhood of years of Yusuf (a.s.), the youthful years of Yusuf (a.s.), and the adult years of Yusuf (a.s.)—with many lessons to be learned in each part. All throughout, we see the miraculous ability of Yusuf (a.s.) to interpret dreams and to foretell the future by the knowledge given to him by Allah.

In Yusuf's childhood, you see discussion in the early part of the chapter and in the late part of the *juz* about the dreams that he would see and how it was interpreted by his father, and the dreams that the prisoners and the king would see and how Yusuf interpreted them. Yusuf (a.s.) even knew what food would come the next day. Jealousy of brothers and jealousy within the family are something real, and sibling rivalry is addressed here in the Qur'an. The hostility can lead a person into making irrational judgements that can push a person further than they initially thought or wanted to go. All of it comes back to Yusuf (a.s.) being prepared for something great. When you are put in hardship and you are put in *fitnah*, it proves your mettle, your goal rises, and you become worthy of it.

Yusuf's transitional story then is that he was given beauty, and a mistress of his home—one who was higher than him in wealth and status and ordered him in menial jobs—attempted to seduce him. This seduction was a great test. He protected himself from immodesty by requesting from Allah, making *du'a* to be imprisoned. This shows the consciousness of Yusuf (a.s.); but it also shows that Yusuf (a.s.) made a *du'a*, that he chose God to give him greater protection. It is at this moment that the dreams of the king come to bear, and Yusuf interpreted them. The king gave Yusuf freedom, and what was destruction, now became an elevation of stature for Yusuf (a.s.).

Juz 12 ends with the woman who accused Yusuf (a.s.) finally admitting her guilt and taking ownership of it. She then repented to Allah (s.w.t.).

JUZ 13

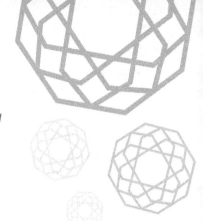

JJuz 13 begins near the middle of Surah Yusuf. This is the moment of awakening. The wife of al-Aziz, who was chasing after Yusuf (a.s.), finally came to terms with the reality that it was her fault. Allah (s.w.t.) quoted her, where her words were very expressive in her remorse, and she returned to Allah in a great *tawbah*.

The king, upon hearing this, knew that Yusuf was imprisoned innocently and yet had remained faithful and patient. He had not misspoken about others nor did he made any false claims about others. He saw Yusuf (a.s.) as a man of trust. Yusuf (a.s.) at the end says, *Allow me an opportunity to assist you and be the guardian over the food source.* This is very important to show that even in a position of weakness, Yusuf (a.s.) comes forward and puts himself up for a level of responsibility and leadership.

From that moment on, Allah transitions quickly into the story of Yusuf (a.s.) having gotten a position of trust, power, and authority on account of the genuineness of his heart. His brothers entered the scene during the seven years of famine. Yusuf (a.s.) recognised them, but they did not recognise him. Never in their wildest dream did they think that a minister of Egypt would be their long-lost, abused brother who was sent away by them.

Yusuf (a.s.) immediately began to ask about the family's condition. He was generous to his brothers but said that he could not give them all that they needed unless he knew about the whole family. Yusuf asked them to bring their other brother, and they returned to their father Ya'qub (a.s.) with that request. At this point, Ya'qub (a.s.) was about to be tried again. All these years, he was missing Yusuf (a.s.) and was praying to Allah for his return; now Allah was going to take yet another son from him—without Ya'qub (a.s.) knowing that it was for his protection. That is one of the greatest lessons that we learn from Surah Yusuf, that in difficulties lies a great measure of success.

Allah was about to take another son of Ya'qub (a.s.), but it would bring relief and happiness in the end. This *surah* discusses jealousy and the importance of keeping prying eyes away; about the increase of test after test; which is a sign of the love of Allah; about Allah showing how Yusuf (a.s.) tested his brothers with the veracity of events, and that they failed the test because they misspoke of Yusuf (a.s.). If the young boy had stolen—which was the ploy that Yusuf (a.s.) used by causing the measuring cup to be placed in his brothers' saddle without them knowing it—he would be taken; it was a way of testing them and saving his young brother from whatever abuse the other brothers may have been planning. In that way, Yusuf (a.s.) put a test on them— what they would do and how would they return to their father Ya'qub (a.s.). It shows you that knowing about Allah (s.w.t.) means having good hope in Allah.

When Ya'qub (a.s.) heard that yet another son had been taken, he said, *I know about Allah that you do not know. I know that Allah is generous, loving and kind to me. Allah will never let me down.*

Allah also speaks about the statement of Yusuf (a.s.) when his brothers finally identified him and knew that he was Yusuf. He said, *The only reason that I was ascended above you, is because surely the one who remains conscious of God, and is pious, righteous in their conduct and is patient, Allah does not lose the account, the favour and the blessing of those who do righteous deeds.*

Immediately after speaking about *taqwa* and *sabr*, Allah (s.w.t.) speaks about *at-tamkin*, which is about gaining authority and prominence in the land. These are all wonderful statements from Allah in the Qur'an to reassure the hearts.

Surah Yusuf ends with the fulfilment of his dream, which had taken decades to come. At the beginning of Surah Yusuf, he said, *I see eleven stars bowing down to me, the sun and the moon subjugated to me.* Then when the time came, his brothers were all subjugated to him, his father and mother were recollected with him, and it was a fulfilment of the dream from Allah. Therefore, dreams do come true even if it is many years later.

The next is Surah Ar-Ra'd, which is a phenomenal *surah* in the Qur'an. It is one of those chapters where Allah (s.w.t.) instils in us His majesty. It has two major overarching themes about *tawhid*: why Allah is central to us and the belief in the Prophet Muhammad (s.a.w.), proving his messengership. But sewn together in that is what Allah asks us to ponder—to understand who He is and why He has sent us the Prophet Muhammad (s.a.w.). *Have they not come to know that what has been sent to you from your Lord is a statement of truth? Or are they going to be like the one who is blinded? Surely only those who ponder over it and remember are those whose hearts are awake.*

In verses 19 till 23, Allah speaks about ten different characteristics that we should embellish within ourselves. What are the signs of those whose hearts are true? They are those who fulfil their covenant to Allah when they made it; they are not those who disband when promises have been made. They are those who connect what Allah has ordered to be connected, maintained, and practised. They are those who have been in awe and humility before their Lord. They are those who not just have that awe of their Lord but they also fearful of the day they will meet Him, a day of accounting for their deeds. They are also those who are patient in seeking the majesty of the face of their Lord. They are patient in doing good deeds, and that is the greatest level of patience we must endure as it is more difficult to be upon truth than it is to stay away from evil. The greatest way to show that you are patient upon truth is that you establish the prayer and give and spend from that which Allah has blessed you with—both in privacy and publicly, making it known so that other people can follow their example. And they wipe away their sinful deeds using their good deeds; they wipe away evil with righteousness in its place.

For them will be the eventual happiness in the final life and happiness and contentment in this life. But the greatest reward is that they will enter Jannah as their final abode. But it is not a blanket statement—it does not mean that just because you enter Jannah, that everyone you love will enter. No. *Only the ones who are righteous from their parents, spouses, and descendants.* And the angel shall enter upon them from every door and say, *Greetings be upon you for the patience that you showed in that worldly life.* That is a phenomenal moment in Surah Ar-Ra'd.

Surah Ibrahim follows that same theme, and it gives the example of Prophet Ibrahim (a.s.) and his patience. It ends with Allah (s.w.t.) speaking about the punishment of disbelief, oppression, and the parable of the good word in comparison to the bad word. It also speaks about the *du'a* of Ibrahim (a.s.): "*Our Lord, forgive me and my parents and the believers the Day the account is established.*"

JUZ 14

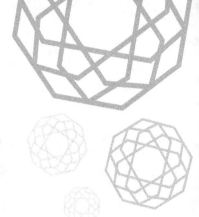

Juz 14 starts at the beginning of Surah Al-Hijr. Surah Al-Hijr is one of those majestic *surah*s. It begins with Allah (s.w.t.) speaking about His vow to protect the Qur'an. *I am The One who has revealed this revelation on to you, and I vow to assure its protection and longevity.* This sets a very decisive role through the Prophet (s.a.w.) that he was undoing years of corruption that have entered by the hands of men and mistranslations and misinterpretations of previous scriptures. But the Qur'an will be kept intact in its native Arabic language, and it will be passed on and protected in the hearts of people, in the *mushaf*, and in the practice of humanity.

Allah also speaks about His magnificence and His presence in the dominion of His creations. He is The One who is irresistible and The One who cannot be contended with. Therefore, He gives this discussion where He speaks about His creations and resurrection. It is as if Allah (s.w.t.) is saying, that for The One who has brought things out of nothing, surely you must understand that He can bring things back in the way and manner that He seeks.

Allah (s.w.t.) speaks of Himself as The Provider. He speaks about *rizq* in a variety of capacities and that *rizq* is something that is not human-induced. So your *rizq* and prosperity, all the economies of the world that we have in one way or another, they originate from divine providence. The rain brings down water, therefore the earth is irrigated and agriculture grows from it. Look into the depths of the earth and you see from the creation of it, the ores that you extract that are the basis of your economies, resources, fossil fuels—all of that in one way or another is beyond human capacity to bring out of nothingness. We are only there to enjoy the blessings of Allah. This is important because the previous *surah*, Surah Ibrahim, ends with Allah (s.w.t.) speaking about *zulm*, corruption. Do not believe those who commit corruption on the earth and oppress others, thinking that Allah is unaware of what they do. Rather, Allah defers it for a day when they will be questioned by Him.

At the beginning of this *juz*, Allah (s.w.t.) speaks about His blessing—do not think that you are so deserving of things. And next chapter, which is also in this *juz*, talks about the blessings of Allah (s.w.t.) and how mankind at times have forgotten their place with their Maker.

In Surah Al-Hijr, Allah also speaks about some of the important stories that He shared with Prophet Muhammad (s.a.w.) to strengthen his heart, to give him a conviction, to show him the right way and that there were great people who were tested by Allah, and that Allah would use the word *glad tidings* for them in a test that was coming. Allah would give glad tidings to Ibrahim (a.s.) about a son that he would be gifted, but, *subhanAllah*, he had to leave the son in the desert in Makkah with his mother, Hajar. That was a great test.

Allah also says in verses 49 and 50, "*Inform My servants that it is I who am the Forgiving, the Merciful. And that it is My punishment which is the painful punishment.*" Allah also tells that He will test us in that regard.

Allah also tells about Lut (a.s.) in great detail and that sexual immorality and other similar or related wrongdoings were dealt with by Allah (s.w.t.) in the most severe way. It is as if the greatest test for Lut (a.s.) is that he was calling his people to purity, but they rejected him on account of that purity. *Muhammad, you are going to call your people to purity and good, and you may be rejected by it, so continue in the right way.*

Allah gives us the final statement to the Prophet (s.a.w.). *O' Muhammad, We know that your heart seizes and is anguished at what they say when they reject the truth and the righteousness you are calling them to; all I ask you to do is to glorify the name of your Lord and maintain your sujud to Me. It is not about whether they believe in you or not; it is whether you have delivered the message or not and whether you maintain a righteous life and maintain your 'ibadah until your yaqin comes.* Yaqin is that your death comes, your life in this world eventually ends, and your certainty arrives.

Then Allah begins Surah An-Nahl. The instruction of Allah has arrived and that Day of Judgement has arrived, but do not be impatient for it. It is as if Allah is saying that *it is already coming, you just do not know it; in your time frame, you are waiting for it; but My orders have already been given.* Everything has been set in motion, the final messenger has been sent, and everything has been decided.

Surah An-Nahl is a powerful *surah* that focuses on the blessings of Allah. Allah speaks about His blessings and that the greatest blessing of them is the Qur'an. Allah mentions this in three places in Surah An-Nahl. Therefore, Allah says, *I have given you these blessings, so have you been thankful?*

Allah speaks about blessings in different ways. He speaks about the sun, the moon, the vegetation, the rain, our mind, our intellect, our faith, the Qur'an, and the spirit of revelation. So what are the blessings mentioned? The creation of men, animals, water, fruits, the earth and the sky, the ocean and the stars; the alternation of the night and the day, and the sun and the moon—all of those area given as signs from Allah.

Then Allah (s.w.t.) tells us that these are blessed things that He has given us in general, followed by specific blessings. He speaks about the blessings in terms of the cattle, honey and the bees, our *rizq*, our spouses, our children, the parable of a person who has been given wealth and a share of influence over others, the parable of being a free man compared to being enslaved and in bondage, the one who is unable to hear and understand compared to the one who has rational thinking and clear-sightedness. All of those are the things that Allah reveals as blessings that He has bestowed upon us.

Then Allah asks us to think critically—to be logical. *Can the One who created be made equal to the one who has not created? How can you make the stone idol equal to The Creator of the heavens and the earth? Can the one who has no faith be equated to the one who has belief? Can the one who has migrated and struggled in the path of God be made equal to the one who has sat back at home and done nothing? Can the One who has created mankind and spread them on the earth be made equal to the one who has brought nothing? Allah* is elevated above all that they estimate of Him.

After transitioning from asking us to think clearly about blessings, He asks us to observe His creations. *Look into the womb of your mother. Look into the creations— the floating and the flying of the bird. Look at the upkeep of even the shadows and the shade that Allah has provided. Look at the clothes that you wear—everything that you have is provided to you by Allah up to this day.* And examples are then given. Allah makes an example of a town that used to believe and then began to disbelief in Allah, and Allah tested them with difficulty.

Finally, Allah gives advice to the Prophet (s.a.w.). *Let people understand this, call them to the path of righteousness, with wisdom, good counsel, and show them the best of your manners.*

JUZ 15

The Qur'an is made and comprised of 30 *juz*. The beginning of Juz 15 is the beginning is Surah Al-Isra'. This is a majestic *surah*. It is a *surah* that gets its name from the night journey. It also has another name: Surah Bani Isra'il (The Children of Isra'il).

The first verse is a declaration by Allah (s.w.t.) of His magnificence. How majestic is He Who transported His servant, Muhammad (s.a.w.), from the Sacred House in Makkah to the Distant Mosque. The Distant Mosque, Masjidil Aqsa, is the second mosque that has been dedicated as a place of worship anywhere on this earth by mankind; the first is in Makkah Al-Mukarramah. Masjidil Aqsa is the first *qiblah* that the believers used to turn to. When they migrated to Madinah, they used to face Masjidil Aqsa until Allah accepted the *du'a* of the Prophet (s.a.w.) to turn his face towards the direction of the Kaabah, which shows the nobility to the Kaabah and our the Prophet (s.a.w.).

Masjidil Aqsa holds an important place for us as Muslims. It is one of those contested cities that has always been under siege and conquest, yet Allah says, *It is a city that I surrounded with My mercy.* The mercy of Allah is sometimes forgotten; it can be found in the hardship He tests us in that requires patience, devotion, and perseverance, ultimately leading us to higher places in Jannah.

This *surah* has a number of different facets. The first of them is about the night journey of the Prophet (s.a.w.). It was a real journey, where he was transported physically and spiritually from Makkah to Jerusalem, and from Jerusalem to the ascension to Allah (s.w.t.). The Prophet (s.a.w.) had a meeting with the prophets there in Jerusalem. They were brought to life and prayed behind him. Many miracles were exchanged and shown to the Prophet (s.a.w.). A lot of what would unfold to his *ummah* was explained to him. It was during his ascension to Allah that he conversed with Him and received the fifty prayers, which were brought down to the five prayers that we perform today.

The second section of the *surah* speaks directly to Bani Isra'il about some of the dysfunctions that they had entered into. It speaks about it through the story of Musa (a.s.) and how far Bani Isra'il at the time of the Prophet (s.a.w.) had strayed from the ideal that was sent to Musa (a.s.). It also speaks about the corruption that they caused in the land. In foretelling, Allah says that they will commit the corruption again, they will return into that mosque again, and they will try to seize it; but eventually, the place is always for the believers.

Then Allah cautions us. *The one who does not want to hold on and restrict their lustful gratification in this life, and does not want to wait till the next life and the happiness it entails; We will give them this worldly life, and We will give them their pleasure. But the one who seeks the next life and works for it in the way that they should with faith and piety; they will see that their hard work will be thanked by Me on the Day of Judgement.* This is an admonition that there is a next life and that you have to work for it and work hard.

From verse 22 until 35, He begins speaking about 20 commandments. He gives many commandments, and from those commandments are not associating partners with Allah, not being disobedient to Allah, not being disobedient to your parents, giving the relatives their rights, giving the needy their rights, being humble with the words you choose and not use vulgar words, spending from your wealth in moderation, and not worrying about your financial future thus taking the life of your young children (infanticides and abortions).

Allah also speaks about not consuming the wealth of the orphans, the fulfilment of promises, measuring things with justice and being equitable, not speaking about Allah any word except that you know it with surety of knowledge, not making any declaration that you have no authority or knowledge of them, and not walking upon the earth in arrogance.

Then Allah gives instructions to Prophet Muhammad (s.a.w.). Near the end of Surah Al-Isra', Allah states that the Prophet (s.a.w.) would be protected from his enemies; that you should say goods word, even to those who use bad words; that Allah will keep the Prophet firm, and Allah will assist him; and that you are to establish the prayers, so that you will arise to a praiseworthy station. Then Allah finalises it by saying that Allah is enough for you.

Next, Allah begins Surah Al-Kahf. It is the *surah* that is recited every Friday by faithful Muslims. The Prophet (s.a.w.) said that the one who recites it is protected from the Dajjal, and when you recite the *surah* from one Juma'ah to the next, it fills the week with light, and it will be a source of light for you on the Day of Judgement.

Surah Al-Kahf has four essential lessons. It speaks about the four great trials that many of us will endure— some of us will have one, two, or three, but not all of us will have all four. The first is a trial in matters of faith. The second is in wealth, prosperity, and greed. The third is in knowledge, practising what you know, and living a life according to the dictates and teachings of revelation. The fourth is in the power of authority, prestige, and governance.

At the end of Juz 15, the first three of those tests manifest themselves in three stories: the story of the people of the Cave—which is how the *surah* gets its name—the story of the man with the two gardens, and the story of Musa (a.s.) with Khidr (a.s.). The fourth story is about Dhulqarnayn, which begins in the next *juz*.

JUZ 16

Surah Al-Kahf has four essential elements, and they revolve around four main tests that human beings are tested with: the tests of faith, of wealth, of knowledge, and of power. Each of them is an arduous test, but combined together, it becomes something that is very difficult to face for a person who is not in tune with the light of revelation.

The first three tests are addressed in the previous *juz*. The people of the Cave are tested in their belief, and they have to hide their faith. They looked for shelter in a cave in order to remove themselves from persecution—they would rather leave their society than lose their faith.

The second test is the test of wealth. There were two neighbours with neighbouring gardens. One of the men thought that what he had was all due to his hard work, his routine system, and his agricultural basis. Allah then caused the garden to become nothing the next morning, and the man then regretted making himself at par with Allah.

The third test is the test of knowledge. Musa (a.s.) assumed that he was the most knowledgeable of Allah's creatures walking the earth, but Allah (s.w.t.) then showed Khidr (a.s.) to Musa (a.s.). Khidr (a.s.) had knowledge that was intimate to Allah that Musa (a.s.) had not received. Knowledge is something that can always be acquired, and for everyone endowed with knowledge, there is always someone who knows more. It is not about how much you know, but how much you practise what you know.

The fourth test, which is mentioned at the beginning of this *juz*, is about Dhulqarnayn, the man who governed two eras or the person of the two horns. It is a story that relates to justice, helping others, and signs of the Day of Judgement. The story also mentions Yakjuj and Makjuj, which are one of ten signs proclaimed by the Prophet (s.a.w.) that all human beings will accept when they emerge later on.

The first lesson we can extract from Surah Al-Kahf is from the story of the people of the Cave, that is, to be steadfast and accepting of the difficulties that Allah tests us with in life. Also, the story teaches us to do the best that we can in facing the tests.

Lesson number two is about being humble and having humility, even when you are blessed with wealth. You have to know that what Allah has given to you, He is also capable of removing it. Thus, we are encouraged to ask Allah to increase for us *barakah*, rather than to have pride and arrogance.

Lesson number three is that the knowledge and wisdom of Allah (s.w.t.) are beyond the human knowledge and ability. That is not just about what you know, but also about how you practise it.

Lesson number four is to use your power and authority to be in the help of others, rather than having others to be at your servitude.

The next *surah* is Surah Maryam. It begins with *Kaf Ha Ya 'Ain Sad.* These are disjointed letters that are miraculous in their nature in the sense that nobody knows their meaning, except Allah and the Prophet (s.a.w.). There are details in the Qur'an that will escape us—we do not have to know what every letter in the Qur'an means for us to believe in its entirety.

Surah Maryam revolves around the conceptualisation of purity. There is the word that relates to purity in the very essence of its title. The name *Maryam* can be translated as the anointed, pure one. In this *surah*, there is also reference to Zakariyya, and his name came from the word *zaka*, which means the purified one. Meanwhile, the name *Yahya* means the one who has a pure life. All of these are allusions to that concept. Purification, which is the underlying theme of this *surah*, includes the purification of the heart, body, clothes, physical proximity, and our intention in worship towards Allah.

There are a number of prophets and messengers mentioned in this *surah*. The solidifying factor between all of the prophets and messengers is family relations. This *surah* is really about parenthood. Zakariyya (a.s.) wanted a son. Maryam (a.s.) was going to be a mother of a son without having had a husband. 'Isa (a.s.) was going to be a son who would grow up without a father; Musa (a.s.) and Harun (a.s.) were two brothers carrying the same message. Ibrahim (a.s.) had to contend with his father not being a believer. Allah further mentions that the prophets were the descendants of Adam (a.s.), Nuh (a.s.), Ibrahim (a.s.), and Ya'qub (a.s.), solidifying relationships about families.

The story about Zakariyya (a.s.) and Yahya (a.s.) is about the acceptance of *du'a*—not to give up, to keep asking for it, and not to be restrained. Meanwhile, it is a test for Maryam that her life was so easy in her worship—Allah blessed her with the angels coming and speaking to her, as well as providing food for her. Yet, her greatest test was the adversity that she had to face and the false accusations that would be made against her.

The miraculous conception of Yahya (a.s.) as well as 'Isa (a.s.) is made equal. Yahya (a.s.) came to a father and a mother who had not had any children, who were beyond the age and physical capacity of carrying a child; yet, by the power of Allah, they conceived and were blessed with a child. It was in the same way as Maryam (a.s.). How could a child be born without a father? As repeated in this *surah*, Allah simply says *Be* and it becomes, by His power.

The next trial was upon Yahya (a.s.). He was martyred, murdered by the people. The people were trying to do the same unto 'Isa (a.s.); however, Allah saved 'Isa (a.s.).

In this *surah* too, we find the concept of *zakah* and *salah* being repeated. Other than that, there are stories about the prophets. Musa (a.s.) and Harun (a.s.) co-operated upon the truth as they called people to good. Isma'il (a.s.) kept his promises to Allah and ordered his family to maintain the *salah* and to give the *zakah*. Idris (a.s.) was elevated to a high status. The angels came to the Prophet (s.a.w.) with the answers from Allah for the questions that were being asked to him.

Meanwhile, the words *Ar-Rahmah* and *Ar-Rahman* are mentioned more than 20 times in Surah Maryam. Look at the places where the words are found in the *surah*—it will give you an insight as to how to earn the mercy of Allah. Also, there are five fruits of *taqwa* mentioned in this *surah*: the love of Allah, protection from a rabid enemy, protection from the *shaytan*, blessings and an increase in *rizq*, and a promise of Jannah.

Surah Maryam ends with the description of the Day of Judgement. Everyone shall enter the Hellfire, except those who are favoured by Allah. Then Allah says that the heavens are likely to rip open and the mountains will crash at the claim that He has taken and begotten a son.

The next chapter in this *juz* is Surah Taha. It chronicles the life of Musa (a.s.), from how he was saved from Fir'awn to his whole lifestyle and everything about him. It has three main sections: the attributes of Allah, including that He is elevated above His 'arsh (Throne), and that Allah is the One who descends the Qur'an upon us; the story of Musa (a.s.) and all of the different elements in it, including how they relate to Fir'awn's magicians, how Allah saved Musa (a.s.) and his people in the migration to Sinai, and how these were given as lessons to Prophet Muhammad (s.a.w.)—*that the truth will set you free, and being a person who follows what is right will lead you to the truth; and that your people may have heard the truth but they can go back into corruption like what happened with the people of Musa (a.s.), who followed and worshipped the golden cow after being saved by*

Allah; and the story of Adam (a.s.), including his test in Jannah. We are also reminded to focus on our family and that patience is the solution in this life. 🕸

JUZ 17

Juz 17 opens with Surah Al-Anbiya. This *surah* takes its name from the many stories of the prophets. It begins with Allah (s.w.t.) warning about the Day of Judgement, which is really the job title of all of the prophets, as they were to give glad tidings of Jannah and admonitions of the Day of Judgement.

Initially, Allah speaks about those who are in the state of heedlessness. *The Judgement Day is arriving, but they are heedless. Therefore, your job, o' Muhammad, is to wake them up and to bring them to this reality. Let them understand three things. First, their accounting is near. Second, I have destroyed many towns, villages, people, dynasties, generations, and cultures that have preceded your culture and your people. Third, even if this destruction does not arrive imminently because you have rejected the messenger—as it happened to other previous nations—and even because of the blessedness of Muhammad being with you that you are not being destroyed, then know that your death is close.* Those are the three levels of warning that Allah gives about the tribulations in the opening verses and in the theme of Surah Al-Anbiya.

In the next section, Allah speaks about the perfection of *tawhid*. It is something that you look at yourself inwardly and outwardly, and you will see that it is a manifestation of the completion of Allah's relationship with humanity. He wants us to identify Him and to know that for everything that is around us, there is a cause—it did not just come out of nothing. The One who has caused all of these is Allah (s.w.t.).

Allah then speaks about different prophets and different messengers. He speaks about the relationship between Musa (a.s.) and Harun (a.s.), and of them being sent to Fir'awn. He speaks about Ibrahim (a.s.) in great detail. Once again, it is about *tawhid*. This is where we find the greatest detail in the story of Ibrahim (a.s.) smashing the idols. When he was asked if he was the one who did it, Ibrahim (a.s.) said it was done by the largest idol. Ibrahim (a.s.) established the argument; *o' Muhammad, your job is to establish the proof on the people of Quraysh.* Therefore, you would see the similitude between Muhammad (s.a.w.) and Ibrahim (a.s.).

Musa (a.s.) is mentioned in relation to legislation and the application of laws, while Ibrahim (a.s.) is mentioned in relation to establishing the rationale of worshipping the One True God.

Allah then speaks about the people of Lut (a.s.), the people of Sodom and Gomorrah, and their destruction. He also speaks about the people of Nuh (a.s.) who resisted him, including his wife and his son, and their eventual destruction. Dawud (a.s.) and Sulayman (a.s.) are also mentioned—how Allah had given both of them knowledge, wisdom, and governance. But Sulayman was given a little bit of an increase, and that is why he was referred to as Sulayman, The Wise King.

Ayyub (a.s.) is then spoken about in detail. One of the places in the Qur'an where the stories of Ayyub are shared is in Surah Al-Anbiya. Here, Allah speaks about how Ayyub (a.s.) was patient and how he persevered in his illness and the difficulties in the losses of his wealth and children. He simply said to Allah, "*Indeed, adversity has touched me, and you are the Most Merciful of the merciful.*"

Allah also speaks about Isma'il (a.s.), Idris (a.s.), Dhulkifl (a.s.), Zakariyya (a.s.), Yahya (a.s.), and 'Isa (a.s.) and his mother, Maryam (a.s.). All of them are mentioned and therefore, this *surah* gets its name from the stories of the prophets.

At the end of the *surah* and all throughout, Allah speaks about *qiyamah*, which returns us to the beginning of the warning that the Day of Judgement is coming. He says, "*On that Day, We will roll up the heavens like a scroll of writings...*" Everything that is created is meaningless to His might and His majesty. The same message was said in books which preceded the Qur'an, in the Psalms of David. The splendidness of Jannah will be inherited by those who work righteous deeds. All this was a reminder to the Prophet Muhammad (s.a.w.) that he was only sent onto mankind to be an expression of Allah's mercy.

The next chapter is Surah Al-Hajj, which is in the same *juz*. Allah (s.w.t.) once again begins a *surah* by speaking about the destruction of the earth and the coming of the Day of Judgement. *O' you who believe, fear your Lord and fear the quaking of the earth—it will be a powerful and magnificent display on that Day.*

Allah then speaks about the creation of humanity from one cycle to the next. This happens in the next *surah* and the next *juz* as well. Allah also debates the disbelievers who do not believe and do not wish to submit to His authority and might. There is also a mention about the relationship between the spirit and the body. We should be the people who live a life that is not just physical, because the human spirit has needs that are beyond that.

In this *surah*, there are two places of *sajdah*. In one of them, Allah (s.w.t.) tells us that all that is in heavens and the earth make *sajdah* to Him—the sun, the moon, the stars, the mountains, the trees, the living creatures, and the people who pledge allegiance to Allah.

Then Allah speaks about *hajj*. In Surah Al-Baqarah, Allah speaks about the ritual aspects of *hajj*, what to do on what day, and so on. But here in Surah Al-Hajj, Allah speaks about the spirit of *hajj*. Allah does not receive the blood of the offering of sacrifice; rather, He receives the piety that you have extended. Allah wants you to come to Him with an open heart, seeking His mercy. It is He who will respond to you.

Allah speaks about the response to those who have lied about Him, about Prophet Muhammad (s.a.w.), about the people of the prophets who had come before— that their end was always tragic. Allah seeks happiness and closure for the *ummah* of Prophet Muhammad (s.a.w.). Allah continues to give evidence of His power and authority, and He speaks of this by giving words directly to the unbelievers. He says that among the signs of *qiyamah* is that there are different types of people: those who will debate the Prophet Muhammad (s.a.w.) without knowledge, those who will worship Allah on the verge of disbelief and then who will come back to belief, and those who believe in Allah (s.w.t.). All these three distinct groups have different remedies that are found in the *surah*. Ultimately, at the end of the day, there are two opposing forces: the people of faith and the people who lack it.

Ibrahim (a.s.) takes a central mission in the story of *al-hajj*. *Proclaim the call to hajj, o' Ibrahim. They will come on their feet, walking, and on all modes of transport to answer the call to Allah.*

The final instruction is to the Muslims, that they have been given permission to defend themselves. They have been ordered to reject all falsities as claimed in previous scriptures that have been corrupted. Those who reject the Qur'an are rejecting their own scriptures, which had the spirit of the Qur'an.

Allah finally mentions to establish our prayers and *zakah*, and to hold on to Him. He is The One who will give victory and strength. 🞑

JUZ 18

Juz 18 begins with Surah Al-Mu'minun. It is a *surah* that is dearly beloved to the believers. Its description is about belief and unbelief, and of the consequences and rewards for either side.

The *surah* begins with Allah listing certain characteristics that the believers have. *Successful are the believers*. They are those who have humility and khushu' in their prayers, abstain from vain and idle talk, give zakah, guard their private relationships and are careful not to fall into sexual misconduct, watchful of their trusts and fulfil their covenants, and guard their prayers (done on time, in the right way, and in the right capacity).

Then Allah transitions to speak about the signs of disbelievers. He does this by speaking about Nuh (a.s.) and other nations that were destroyed. The people of Nuh were rebellious people who had arrogance in them and were unwilling to conform to what easily could be recognisable as a statement that calls them to purity and the path to faith. Allah speaks about His blessings upon them and them not being worthy of the blessings because of their rejection.

Other generations who followed after that continued in disbelief, except a few who came to belief. Allah wants us to be from those who are believers. Allah then shares more signs of the believers. They are those who have an awe of Allah (s.w.t.) and His magnificence, have a firmness of faith, do not make *shirk*, give their fear only to Allah, and are cognizant of their relationship with their Maker, and how they live with other people impacts that relationship with The Almighty.

The disbelievers, on the other hand, are given two primary characteristics. They are those who are arrogant, proud, unwilling to accept the truth, and unwilling to come to a path, even to a compromise of what they know was right and what they know was good, simply because it has come from a particular messenger. Whenever the messengers would come to them, they would reject faith on account of their arrogance and pride.

The second characteristic is that they are wasteful of time until the moment of regret. They do not care about the number of years that Allah has blessed them with wealth and health. On the Day of Judgement, they will say, *O Allah, return us to the life that we will do righteous deeds, give us another chance. We have missed out this time. Allow us one more opportunity.* Allah says, *No, rather it is just the word that you say.* In another place, Allah says that if they were to be returned, they would do exactly the same and make the same bad choices.

Then Allah speaks about consequences on the day when the trumpet of the Day of Judgement will be blown, and everyone will know that the matter has been decided. Deeds will be weighed. People will then begin to have conversations about the regrets that they have. The people of Jannah will be proud, and the people of the Hellfire will be worried. Success and belief are mentioned concurrently in this *surah*. Therefore, the disbelievers can never find success.

The next chapter is Surah An-Nur (The Light). This *surah* speaks about social conventions: what is moral and what is immoral, especially in relation to sexuality and sexual misconduct; the importance of guarding the tongue and how we use it; chastity; and honouring each other's relationship.

The worst evil that a human being can do is fornication because one allows his or her base desire to take over. On the first page of this *surah*, there are punishments and consequences to that effect that are listed. Accusations against chaste women are as severe as committing a sexual act of misconduct. The rulings of *li'an* are established—if someone suspects their spouse of having committed adultery, what are the ways of taking an oath to this.

The incident of 'Aisha (r.a.) is outlined in the second page of the *surah*. It is also featured in the Sahih Al-Bukhari and Sahih Muslim. It is directly spoken about in the *surah*, and her innocence is declared by Allah from above the seven heavens.

The etiquettes of modesty are also outlined in this *surah*. Do not enter someone's house without permission. Keep your gaze lowered from that which is enticing and that which you do not have the right to see. Do not openly display your beauty in a way of vulgarity to attract attention from others. Unmarried people should try to get married as soon as they are able, and people should try to assist them in getting married. Do not compel those who are captive into immodest dealings. Do not marry people who practise prostitution as a mean of living.

Then Allah speaks about His guidance. The imagery of the light of Allah is used as the source of guidance. Allah is The Light of the heavens and the earth. It is one of the most commented verses—*I recommend for you to listen to the tafsir of it by Dr. Yasir Qadhi.*

Believers are those who benefit from the light of Allah. He gives the parable of the unbelievers as having one of two things: either they see a mirage—something that they think is right, but when they get to it, it is nothing; or they are in another state—complete darkness, that if they were to put their hand in front of their face, they cannot even see it.

The third section of the *surah* is about the signs of belief. Everything claims belief in Allah and proclaims purity of worship of Allah. Some will turn back from sinfulness and come back to Allah. Repentance is always open for a believer who has defiled himself in the sight of Allah and then returned to Him seeking forgiveness.

Those who truly believe are those who give their *zakah*. That is one of the first things that is mentioned. The believers establish their *salah* as well as have righteous actions particularly with their society and the people they live with.

Allah then speaks about the needs to protect children and those who are in bondage. He also speaks about the rules for the elderly. He speaks about the call of the Prophet (s.a.w.)—to call people to that light of Allah and to that which will enrich them in life.

The closing of the *juz* begins with Surah Al-Furqan, which is the 25th chapter of the Qur'an. Al-Furqan means the criteria, the divider between right and wrong, good and bad, *halal* and *haram*, *tawhid* and *shirk*.

In this *surah*, Allah speaks about the importance of praising The Almighty and identifying Him before the Day of Judgement where the *furqan* will be made for us and we will be divided into two groups: the believers and the unbelievers. It is the initial opening of Surah Al-Furqan that is found in the last pages of Juz 18.

JUZ 19

Juz 19 begins in Surah Al-Furqan. Allah (s.w.t.) determines *al-furqan* as a criterion between right and wrong, good and bad, *halal* and *haram*, *tawhid* and *shirk*. In the opening, Allah speaks about those who have a great deal of sorrows and those who have challenged the Messenger of Allah and strayed away from His path. *You will find the one who has wronged themselves bite onto their hand on the Day of Judgement. They will say, I wish I had followed the messenger, I wish I had not strayed away from this path of truth.*

Allah (s.w.t.) is The One who has shaped everything and brought everything into existence. In this *surah*, Allah speaks about the beauty of the Qur'an. He uses the examples of Musa (a.s.) and Harun (a.s.), as well as of Nuh (a.s.). Allah also speaks about the consequences of those who have left their path and not being from those who are righteous.

Towards the end of this *surah*, Allah (s.w.t.) speaks about everything that He has created around us. *Glorious is Allah who has made the constellations in the heavens, the moon which reflects the light of the sun.* This powerful statement is scientifically accurate as well. This is also a place in the Qur'an where you will make *sajdah*.

And then Allah tells us about the characteristics of those who are the glorious servants of The Lord of Mercy. They are those who walk the earth with humility, avoid arguments with the ignorant, make *du'a* in the depth of the night in the standing of the prayer and in sujud, make *du'a* after worship, ask and beg of their Lord for freedom from the punishment of the Hellfire, seek to be in the state of moderation in their expenses without being extravagant nor withholding, do not associate partners with Allah, do not kill a soul other than that which has been ordered by God, do not commit sexual immorality, do not witness falsehood, pass by vain things and sinful practices with a refinement (they do not turn their gaze toward frivolity), witness unto mankind the truth of scripture and the truth of faith, do not turn away when the Qur'an is recited upon them, and invoke Allah for themselves and their families.

That is how Surah Al-Furqan comes to an end. The *surah* that comes immediately after it is Surah Asy-Syu'ara' (The Poet). However, this *surah* is not about a poet. Rather it includes verses at the end of it that speak about those who lead people astray with jest and the frivolities of worldly life. This *surah* is very much focused on the believers, those who make good choices, and the unbelievers, those who choose a path that strays from Allah. The one who wishes to believe will believe, and the one who wishes to stray will continue to live that life, unashamed.

Many prophets are mentioned in Surah Asy-Syu'ara'. Allah (s.w.t.) answers the accusations that were levelled towards them. Those who practise idolatry, Allah answers it through Ibrahim (a.s.). Those who practise wickedness and sexual misconduct, Allah answers it through Lut (a.s.). Those who are willing to eat and consume the wealth of the orphan and mistreat people financially, there is the example of Shu'ayb (a.s.) and his people. Those who do not want to submit to an authority, there is Fir'awn and Musa (a.s.). All of them are mentioned in this *surah*.

Allah then speaks about those who have redemption, those who become aware, such as Fir'awn's magicians who woke from their delusions and came to a realisation that the power of Allah is not like the power that they tried to bewitch people's eyes with. Rather they saw that the miracles brought by Musa (a.s.) were from God. They turned to Allah in worship in an immediate regret and sorrow of their previous sin.

While on the run from Fir'awn and his army, Musa (a.s.) was confronted by Bani Isra'il. They said, *You have led us into destruction. We are going to die in this water. Fir'awn is pursuing us!* He replied, *No, rather my Lord is with me. He will guide me to the right place and the right way.* He spoke about the firmness of faith and conviction.

Allah (s.w.t.) speaks about Ibrahim (a.s.). There is a powerful *du'a* of Ibrahim (a.s.) in this *surah*. He said, *Give me a good mention in the generations to come.* That is one of the reasons we recite his name in our prayer. Ibrahim (a.s.) asked, *Give me, o' my Lord, a pure heart on the Day of Judgement where only those who have healthy hearts will be given success.* He also made a beautiful *du'a*, *Forgive my father, he was wrongly led.* This *du'a* was made to his father who attempted to kill Ibrahim (a.s.). He stopped making that *du'a* after his father died in the state of *kufr*.

Allah ends the *surah* by discussing the poets who lead away those who have a heart that is desirous of the frivolities of this worldly life, who are not focused on the next life, and do not take seriously the life that they have been blessed by Allah. There are differences between poetry and the verses of the Qur'an. The Qur'an descended with a trustworthy angel, in pure Arabic language that cannot be altered and translated. Arabic is the only language of the Qur'an. The *shaytan* has no interference in the Qur'an, and there is no poetry in it.

The Qur'an is non-terrestrial—not from the Prophet (s.a.w.) but from Allah.

The final section of Juz 19 is Surah An-Naml (The Ants). In this *surah*, Allah speaks about guidance, the people of belief, the Qur'an as the ultimate source of news and guidance, the disbelievers who are wasting their actions by following other than the Qur'an, and Musa (a.s.) who spoke to Allah and asked for guidance, and it was given to him.

Allah then tells us about Dawud (a.s.) and Sulayman (a.s.). Surah An-Naml has a large section on Sulayman (a.s.), which is where the *surah* gets its name. It is when Sulayman (a.s.) heard the ant speak. *O ants, hide! Sulayman and his troops are coming. Go enter your home, so they do not trample on you without knowing!* Sulayman (a.s.) smiled, and he was amused at the ant's authority over others. He understood the language of animals. The incidents of the ants and the *hud-hud* (the hoopoe bird) are made reference to.

The *hud-hud* was travelling far into the regions of Yemen. It saw that there were people prostrating to the sun rather than Allah. *How dare they not worship Allah?* Sulayman (a.s.) then sent a letter through the *hud-hud* to the Queen of Sheba, calling to Allah, and she came to visit. When she entered into Sulayman's magnificent chamber, she thought that the glass floor was water—it was something that she had never seen. She then knew that it was a miracle from Allah and fully submitted herself to Him.

In this *surah*, Allah tells us about the might of the angels when they assisted Sulayman (a.s.) and that Sulayman has power and dominion over the *jinn*. All of these are themes that are found in the early part of Surah An-Naml.

JUZ 20

We resume with the next *juz* near the end of Surah An-Naml. This *surah* speaks about the importance of purifying our intentions with Allah (s.w.t.). Allah then shows that just because we have good intentions, it does not mean that we will be left unharmed. Allah gives the example of Lut (a.s.).

Lut (a.s.) was a person of purity, and this was acknowledged by those who were his opponents, who seek to cause wickedness, corruption, and sexual immorality on this earth. One of the underlying themes in it is that those of righteousness will not be tolerated by those of immorality.

Allah then gives five rhetorical questions in this *surah*. It is a way of laying down the foundations of our faith and re-establishing our *tawhid* and *aqidah*. Allah puts those questions from verse 59 to 64. *Who is it that created the heavens and the earth? Who is it that brings down the water? Who is it that causes your vegetation to grow? Who is it that has provided you with all these luxuries? Who is the one who answers the one who is in need and distressed, other than Allah?*

The *surah* ends with vivid descriptions of the Day of Judgement. It brings to recount some of the major signs that will happen before it, such as the emergence of the beast that will roam the land. Allah says that the one who does righteous deeds shall find their reward, and the one who does not will be treated as a criminal on the Day of Judgement.

The next *surah* is Surah Al-Qasas. The underlying theme of this *surah* is to quell the anguish of the believers who are oppressed. The believers saw all around them the tyranny that is happening in Makkah, the Quraysh mishandling them and abusing them. Allah sends this *surah* to the Prophet (s.a.w.) and his *ummah* at their moment of weakness. *Look, the ascension will always be for those of faith. And I wish to show favour upon those who were treated in oppressive ways upon the earth. I will raise them to be leaders for mankind, and they will inherit the land.*

Allah speaks about five different categories of tyranny in the *surah*. First, the unjust ruler— in the form of Fir'awn. In Surah Al-Qasas, there are the narratives of all the stories of Musa (a.s.) and Bani Isra'il. Second, the oppressive minister—in the form of Haman, who was the chief *wazir* (vizier) of Fir'awn. Third, the deviant clergy—the people of faithfulness who led people astray. The example is the magicians who were called by Fir'awn to establish his dominance on weak-minded people. Fourth, the merciless military—they were used as soldiers by Fir'awn to condemn and murder the young children of Bani Isra'il. And fifth, the evil businessman—the one who is willing to sell his soul for the pleasures of the *dunya*. The one who does not look towards the next day. He deals with people in economic injustice and impunity. This is portrayed in Qarun.

These five are the hallmarks of any deviant society, and any time you see corruption in the earth, it is once again a resumption of that Pharaonic mindset. This is what is given to the Prophet (s.a.w.) and us through the Qur'an. Allah wishes to show us that we are to be patient in enduring trials and leading ourselves to a path of righteousness.

Another important topic in this *surah* is women. Here, Allah (s.w.t.) gives powerful examples of influential women. The mother of Musa (a.s.), for example, had a determination and faced up against the army of Fir'awn who had come to kill her child. She was unwilling to just surrender her child the way hundreds of other women of Bani Isra'il did. In her dream, she saw that she was to build a basket and put Musa in it.

The second most important woman in Musa's life was his sister. She was ordered to watch Musa (a.s.), and she saw that the woman who drew Musa (a.s.) from the water could not find someone to breastfeed him. So she told the woman that she would bring someone who could. She was quick-witted, intelligent, thoughtful, and knew how to handle herself on her feet.

The third reference to women is of the two young ladies who stood in their father's place, herding the sheep, doing the men's job in their society at that time. They did it with ethics and without compromising themselves.

Another important theme is the concept of redemption. After unintentionally killing someone, Musa (a.s.) was able to redeem himself by asking Allah for His forgiveness and His favour. These are all underlying themes that we find in the *surah*.

Allah also speaks about Qarun. He was from Bani Isra'il, but he sold himself and his people to make wealth. He received a lot of money at the expense of those who lived by him and needed his support. But what did it get him in the end? He became a person of arrogance and pride. It led him away from the path of Allah. Finally, Allah opened the earth to swallow Qarun, figuratively and physically. Qarun was a person who had no weight—a person who was not even worthy for the earth to carry his weight, even though the weight of his gold took many men to carry.

At the end of this *juz* is Surah Al-Ankabut. This *surah* speaks about *fitnah*—the tests, trials, and tribulations. Allah says, "*Do the people think that they will be left to say, 'We believe' and they will not be tried? But We have certainly tried those before them...*" Allah made this known to those who were truthful and those who were patient in their claim of being faithful. So if you say you are a believer, know that you are going to be tested by Allah. That test is something that is going to shake you as it shook the people before you.

Allah also speaks about the importance of family, and that the tests of all of the prophets came in different ways. Everyone who calls to a path of truth is tested in the way of *fitnah*. This is one of the lessons given to the Prophet (s.a.w.) and the *sahabah*. *If you are going to call to truth, I am going to test you in one of these ways. The test is either in your family* (like Lut [a.s.] and Nuh [a.s.]) *or in your physical being, or by depriving you of your luxuries, or in your wealth, or in the longevity of your da'wah.*

Then Allah gives the solution near the end of the *juz* where He says, *Those who have made their jihad, who struggled in calling to Us, in establishing this truth with patience—we will lead them to the path that leads them to Our happiness.* ❀

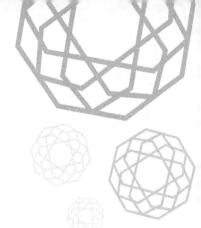

JUZ 21

Allah (s.w.t.) opens this *juz* in Surah Al-Ankabut, by asking us as believers and the Prophet (s.a.w.) as our leader to debate the people of the book, to speak to them with sound argument and with ethics and good manners, and to say to them that our Lord and their Lord is one. They may believe different things about Allah and we may hold Allah to be different, but that the Lord we both worship is one and the same.

Then Allah asks us to look into the cosmos, to look into the blessings that He has set for us, and to recognise that everything ultimately is by His power.

Surah Al-Ankabut puts a finality to the concept of *shirk*—that life is a test, that we are to be obedient to those who are in authority over us (our parents in particular), that we should be suspicious of ourselves entering into a level of hypocrisy, and that we have to be very careful from joining in anything in worship or acts of service that is ritual and spiritual for anything other than Allah. This is given in terms of the stories of the prophets, Ibrahim (a.s.), Lut (a.s.), and Shu'ayb (a.s.); and of the punishment that descended upon their people who disobeyed; and of the salvation granted to the ones who had given themselves over to Allah.

The next *surah* is Surah Ar-Rum. Allah (s.w.t.) says, "*The Romans have been defeated.*" They were the people of the Book; therefore, the Muslims had a greater allegiance and love for them. The Persian army who defeated them were aligned with the Quraysh. This somewhat upset the Muslims, but then Allah gave them the glad tidings that they will come back to victory. Allah shows that He will give victory to whom He chooses and whom He wills.

Allah sets this *juz* into three important sections. He speaks about His signs to humanity, the commands that He asks of them, and the blessings that are received in return. Allah asks us to look within ourselves, to look at the creation of men, at the creation of the heavens and the earth, at the differences of our languages, at the parables of life and death, at the alternation of nights and days, and so on. All these are signs of those who have an awoken consciousness.

Allah then sets it with the concept of *fitrah*—to be steadfast upon that natural disposition all human beings know that something is causing what we do not understand. There is someone that brought something out of nothingness, and it is Allah. He says, *"Do not cause corruption on the earth."* Anytime you see anything out of imbalance on the earth or anything that is not the way it should be, know that it is by what men's hand have earned. Therefore, Allah asks us to return to that natural state of *fitrah*, which is leaving things as they should be, in the capacity and in the balance and harmony that they are destined for. How do you do this? By enjoining what is good, forbidding what is evil, and having faith in Allah. This is the solution that is offered by Allah (s.w.t.).

Allah talks to us about not associating partners with Him, being regular in establishing our prayers, giving the rights to our relatives in particular and the poor in general, not to be from those who partake in *riba*, paying our *zakah* regularly, making sure that we have a share of our wealth to the poor, and recognising that if we do not obey these commands, destruction does follow in this life and in the next life.

Allah asks us to reflect on the grandeur of His majesty in the small acts that He asks of us. Not to focus on what we are doing, but on the magnificence of The One we are worshipping. We must know that these acts of worship have a direct correlation to the blessings that we receive. The blessings can be in forms of rain, the messengers that were sent to us, the Qur'an, the guidance, and the favours of Allah to mankind. The blessings will not end as long as a believer remains devoted.

The next *surah* is Surah Luqman. The *surah* is named after a historic figure, Luqman the wise (*al-hakim*). He was a person who lived in Nubia, a dark-skinned man, a slave owned by another human being. However, his great enslavement was to Allah (s.w.t.), which made even kings bow before Luqman's advice.

Surah Luqman basically begins with a discussion on who are the righteous ones and what are the things that allow them to be righteous. Allah then juxtaposes this against those who are heedless. The heedless are those who enjoy the sinful merriment and frivolity of the lewd things in life. They enjoy that which distracts them from their worship of Allah.

In the second page of the *surah*, Allah begins to mention the advice of Luqman to his son. This was a counsel of a loving father to a son. *My son, first and foremost, do not take partners in your worship of Allah. It is the greatest injustice. Do not be from those who think that they can hide from Allah, even if it is a small mustard seed, in the depth of the earth; Allah will bring it. My son, establish prayer, enjoin what is good, forbid what is evil, and know the consequence of that is that you must be patient on what will befall you. Do not turn your cheek and have arrogance; you are not going to be a person who is going to be able to split the earth in half. You are not a person of substance. You are nothing but a creation of Allah. So know your place in life.*

Then it transitions in Allah giving us insight into what we should hear in that advice of Luqman: to not take partners in the worship of Him, to endure in our patience in the love of Allah, to invite others to that which is good, and to fear Allah.

The last two verses of the *surah* are terrifying. *O' mankind, fear your Lord, and know that there is a day where no one will be benefited with anything—no son will be able to help a father and no father will be able to help his son, except by the order of Allah.*

The final section of the *juz* is Surah As-Sajdah and Surah Al-Ahzab. Surah As-Sajdah has a *sajdah* in it, and Allah speaks to us about the origin of men, the creation of Adam (a.s.) and Iblis, and the long-standing battle. Allah also reminds us of the night prayers, that there is no reward that can be equal to it in this life. Allah says that *iman* can be raised on account of two things. We can be leaders to others when we demonstrate patience and we have certainty in faith.

Surah Al-Ahzab (The Confederates) has its name from one of the battle lead by the Prophet (s.a.w.), where all the confederate tribes of the Quraysh and those around them came to attack Madinah. For a month they laid siege to it, and that was when a trench was dug in Madinah to defend against incoming armies.

At the beginning of the *surah*, Allah orders the Prophet (s.a.w.), *O Messenger of Allah, be mindful and conscious of Allah.* Therefore, you can see that the path to being saved from gathering forces is in the consciousness of Allah.

Finally, Allah says that true men are those who fulfil their covenant to Allah (s.w.t.).

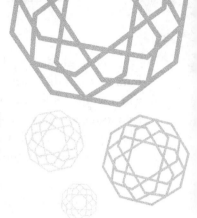

JUZ **22**

Surah Al-Ahzab is featured prominently in Juz 22. It is one of those chapters where Allah (s.w.t.) instils in us a level of gratefulness after difficulty.

The Prophet (s.a.w.) was surrounded by enemies, and Allah gives favour upon him and speaks about his status. Allah describes the Prophet (s.a.w.) to the believers that he was close to them and that Allah knows the Prophet (s.a.w.) has a love for the believers. Therefore, in return, He advises us to be from those who take the Prophet's decisions and his verdicts as law and to be from those who understand that he is a witness over us, a giver of good news, a forbidder evil, a warner and a caller to Allah, and a lamp in the darkness whose light radiates beyond him.

This *surah* explains to us the etiquettes that we must show to the Messenger of Allah (s.a.w.). There is a beautiful verse in this *surah* that says, "*Indeed, Allah confers blessing upon the Prophet, and His angels (ask Him to do so). O you who have believed, ask (Allah to confer) blessing upon him and ask (Allah to grant him) peace.*" It also speaks about the virtues of the family of the Prophet (s.a.w.)—his children, his grandchildren, his wives.

Allah warns us about the consequence of being distant from the Prophet (s.a.w.) or harming other prophets. Towards the end of the *surah*, Allah says, *O' you who believe, do not be harmful to your prophets as those who came before you were harmful to Musa.*

Surah Al-Ahzab is also about the battle of Ahzab. The good news is that Allah sent forces that were unseen—the angels were there to assist the believers towards victory. It also mentions the conquest of Bani Qurayzah.

It speaks directly to the wives of Prophet Muhammad (s.a.w.) to be of a high standard and a pillar within the communities. The order of the veil was established in Surah Al-Ahzab. *O' Prophet of God, say to your wives, to your daughters, and to the women of the believers, to clothe themselves with the jilbab.* All of these are found in the *surah*, plus a few legislations that relate to divorce and remarriage and so on.

The next *surah* is Surah Saba'. It is about Allah's bounty and favours that are changed as a recompense of misdeeds and disobedience. The Prophet (s.a.w.) was given this prophetic guidance to be appreciating of the blessings of Allah in this life so that they can be extended, protected, and be shared with others.

Allah speaks about those who are governed and those who are governors. Each of them has a right over the other, and both are a reflection of one another. Therefore, when you do not like what you see in a society, it begins with you looking inwardly to bring about that change. It is one person who becomes a collective that can bring about the change. All of these are the underlying themes in Surah Saba'.

No obedience should be given in matters of lewdness, sinfulness, and deviance from a path of truth. *Istighfar* is one of the things that heal us. These are things that should be pondered by all of us in our relationship with Allah.

Surah Saba' is a powerful *surah* that tells about a city that changed in its faithfulness to Allah. The people disbelieved in the blessings of Allah; therefore, the blessings were taken away from them. The people were made to taste hunger and thirst as a consequence. The people also began to feud with one another, for they did not see the mistakes within themselves but blamed others instead. That's something we see in society today.

The next chapter is Surah Fatir. It opens with Allah speaking about His angels and His creation of them in their massive beauty. Then Allah speaks about His *rahmah*, His mercy. That it is only Allah who spreads His mercy, and it is only Allah who can confine it. Thus, it becomes an important process for you and me to deal with Allah in a way that gains His mercy.

Allah also addresses the purpose of creation in this *surah. The angels were created without choice; you have a choice, o' mankind.* Allah also speaks about the deception of the *shaytan* and his allure of this worldly life to lead us away from Allah. He speaks about the weakness that is found within us as human beings: we have a dependency on Allah, and if we do not recognise it, we become weaker. He speaks about righteous deeds, that they are for our own benefit and not something that benefits Allah.

Allah gives comparisons between the one who is blind and the one who can see, between darkness and light, between the one who is in the shade and the one under the sun, between the one who is alive and the one who has died. All of these are the similitudes of faith and the lack of it.

Allah responds in different ways to us at different times. We are people who are in a trade with Allah. You are in commerce with Allah. You are buying and selling your soul in that which is righteousness and seeking that which is pleasing to Allah. All of those are overarching themes that we find in Surah Fatir.

The next is Surah Yasin. There are a number of hadith that have been mentioned in relation to this *surah*. Many of the hadiths are weak and do not have authentic chains of narration. But the ones that are authentic do establish its primary role within our belief system as Muslims. It seeks to fulfil two important processes. First, it is confirming that Prophet Muhammad (s.a.w.) as a true messenger of Allah, what his role is, and what the roles of the prophets before him were. Second, it is confirming that the resurrection is a reality. There will be a day when we will stand in front of our Creator and will be asked how we lived our lives.

The name of Surah Yasin comes from its first two letters: *Ya* and *Sin*. These letters have been made as a name for the Prophet (s.a.w.) because it is as if it is speaking directly to him, although there is no record of this being stated by the Prophet (s.a.w.). The *surah* has been given other descriptions by the *'ulama*. It has been called *Al-Mudafi'ah* (the one that defends you), *Al-Qadiyah* (the one that settles matters with Allah), and

Al-Mu'ammimah (the one that is overwhelming in its comprehensive dealings and nature).

There are three important sections of the *surah*: the message of Prophet Muhammad (s.a.w.) is true and Allah will protect him, the deeds are written, and Allah knows what we say.

In this *surah*, Allah gives an example of a man who, at his death, saw the blessings of life and said, *I wish my people whom I am leaving behind knew what I see now and the blessing that Allah has destined because of my faith and belief in Him.* There were three messengers sent to these people, but no one believed in them except this humble man.

Finally, it is about the afterlife, which is the beginning of the next *juz*.

JUZ 23

Allah begins Juz 23 in Surah Yasin, where He has confirmed to us the trueness of the message of the Prophet (s.a.w.) and that he is protected and given assistance divinely by Allah. There is also the confirmation that resurrection is real, and our account will be with Allah, The Most High.

In this *surah*, Allah (s.w.t.) gives a vivid example of Asif ibn Wa'il who came to the Prophet (s.a.w.) while holding a bone in his hand. He proceeded to break it, threw the pieces to the Prophet (s.a.w.), and said, *How can Allah bring this back to life?* Allah responds with, *Say to him: The One who created in the first place is The One who can bring it back.*

Then Allah (s.w.t.) gives us an understanding of His dominion over all that exists—that He is The Only one who is in sole control. Even the sun, the moon, and the celestial bodies move in accordance with the precise plan that Allah has set for them. There is no chaos in it. All of these are mentioned in this *surah*.

Haven't I told you, o' mankind, not to worship shaytan—not to give your allegiance to him? Worship only Allah. That is the straight path that leads to righteousness. Allah then speaks about the final destination—Jannah, its beauty and blessings, and how we can get there.

The next *surah* is Surah As-Saffat. This *surah* goes along the same theme as Surah Yasin. It mentions Allah being The Originator in the creation, and thus the Day of Judgement is in His dominion. To Him, all of us will return.

Even with that knowledge, there are many of those who, when it is said to them, *Worship The One true God*, they have this pride, arrogance, and unwillingness in them to bow down to the majesty of Allah. Therefore, Allah talks about His creations: the angels and their attributes, the sky, the stars, the signs in the constellations, and the miracles that have been set around us.

Allah then speaks about the Day of Judgement. One announcement, one order from Allah, and it will be done. The disbelievers on that day will blame each other. The people of Jannah and the people of the Hellfire will be made clear. There will be this ongoing debate between the two groups shown and broadcasted by Allah.

Next, Allah speaks about the different messengers that were sent to people, and how those who disbelieved in the messengers had different ways of disbelieving—but their outcome was the same. The people disobeyed Nuh (a.s.), Ibrahim (a.s.), Musa (a.s.), Harun (a.s.), Ilyas (a.s.), Lut (a.s.), and Yunus (a.s.); all of them had the same consequence even though their acts of disobedience and the reasons they did not believe in the messengers and in the path of God were different. Allah puts some equation between them.

Allah speaks about the people of Jannah versus the people of Jahannam, and He gives us different signs. Nuh (a.s.) called to Allah for many years, yet very few accepted his call. Ibrahim (a.s.) called to Allah, and the story of the idols is prominently shown. There are three different things that are described about Ibrahim (a.s.): his young days growing up with his father and his rejection of idolatry, how he smashed the idols and how lied to his father and his people about them, and finally the trial that he and his son Isma'il (a.s.) went through. It is as if Allah is saying, *Your father wanted to kill you, o' Ibrahim, because of his commitment to his false god—he threw you into the fire. Can you show that same level of commitment to Me? Slaughter your son.* Therefore, we see that perfect symmetry; as you are a test for others, others will be a test for you.

The next *surah*, Surah Sad, is a mesmerising chapter, and in it is a *sajdah*. Surah Sad is about unveiling the doubts that people have. It tells us that the prophets are a test to mankind. Also, we can see different reasons that people stray. One of them is arrogance. The other is that they assume it is just an illusion or a fraud, and they accuse the prophets of wizardry, magic, and lies. And as for others—because they only follow what their forefathers practised. So if the people before them did not practise it, they therefore are not going to do any different from their forefathers. All of these are different examples portrayed in Surah Sad.

Allah then speaks about prophets who were given different tests. This *surah* emphasises that even the life of a prophet is a test. All of us will have different tests. Dawud (a.s.) has a test. His test was a magnificent test. The two angels who climbed into his prayer house tested him with questions.

The test of Sulayman (a.s.) was the finery of the worldly life. *I have shown love in the indulgence and luxury of this worldly life, and it almost made me forget the worship of my Lord.*

The test Ayyub (a.s.) was loss after loss, but he had the patience to endure the test and not making his *du'a* to Allah hurriedly, to ask Allah for relief. *I answered to Ayyub the moment he made du'a to Me.*

The tests of Ibrahim (a.s.), Ishaq (a.s.), and Ya'qub (a.s.) are all mentioned in this *surah*, as are the tests of Isma'il (a.s.), Ilyasa' (a.s.), and Dhulkifl (a.s.). Allah tells us the saving grace for all of them was one thing, and that is *sabr*—to endure with patience and love.

This *surah* centres around dispute and resolution. All of the different tests of the prophets revolve around disputes that the people had. Our greatest dispute, the one with whom we are vying with the most, is our own soul. You are in charge of yourself, and you will be questioned about it. So do not listen to *shaytan*.

Allah ends Surah Sad by reminding us of the trial of Adam (a.s.), which was Iblis. Iblis used Adam's inner self and inner desires to live forever, to be in prosperity, and to be like the angels that surrounded him.

Surah Az-Zumar begins in this *juz*. In this *surah*, Allah speaks about the purity of intention and the purity of worship—*ikhlas*. Allah says plainly to the Prophet (s.a.w.), *Tell them, o' Muhammad, you have been ordered to worship Me with sincerity of worship, singling me out.* This *surah* is an amazing *surah* in its beauty of showing us the importance of being sincere and loving of our Creator and Maker.

This *surah* tells us that the Qur'an is a cure to that which is in the heart. Those who have true sincerity to Allah are moved by it and its words. Those who are righteous are those who hear the word of the Qur'an and follow its most correct. Those whom Allah has opened his chest and given him faith in his heart is the ones who see with the light of faith, which is the light directed by the Qur'an.

JUZ 24

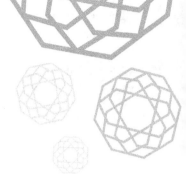

This *juz* continues at Surah Az-Zumar. It is one of those *surahs* that highlight the importance of sincerity in commitment to Allah (s.w.t.). The *surah* explains the need that mankind has in *tawhid* and submission to the Oneness of Allah, verifying Him as The Only One who is worthy of worship, and being sincere in every pursuit of worship we have towards Him.

It is also a condemnation of those who make *shirk*. Allah (s.w.t.) says that their conceptualisation is in error. *To worship something that you believe brings you closer to the Ultimate Creator—when you ask them who created the heavens and the earth, they say Allah. Then why worship anything minor when you can have immediate access to Allah?*

Allah ends the *surah* by saying, *Do not despair. If you have made errors in your past, you can always reform and come back to the truth. You can always become a better person.* Allah speaks directly to the believers, *O' my servants who have wronged and committed atrocities against your own soul, do not despair in the mercy of Allah, for that is a sign of sinfulness and disbelief.*

Allah then tells us that He forgives all sins. It does not matter how many there are, how large they are, or what type they are. Allah is *Al-Ghaffar*, *Al-Ghafur*, and *Al-Ghafir*. The next chapter in this *juz* is Surah Ghafir. It is almost as if Allah is leading us to this conclusion—that He is The Forgiver.

Allah continues by mentioning that there will be two main groups on the Day of Judgement. There will be a group of the people of Jannah and a group of the people of the Hellfire. For the people going to Jannah, the gates of Jannah are laid open for them. *Enter this Jannah, as you have done really well.* The angels that surround the *'arsh* of *Ar-Rahman* will greet them and honour them on that day. On the other hand, for the people of deviance, it is the gates of Jahannam that will be laid open for them. It will call and beckon them to the punishment and the wrath of Allah.

We then come to Surah Ghafir. It is the first of the *Ha Mim surahs*. It is the *surah* where Allah says it is He who is The Forgiver of sins and He is The One who accepts your return to Him. Nevertheless, He is The One who is severe in punishment. None can exceed and go past Him. He is infinite in His mercy, His love, His compassion, His knowledge, and everything about Him. Recognise that none is worthy of worship but He (s.w.t.).

Surah Ghafir continues in that theme of Allah's forgiveness and His Love for us. Then, Allah gives us a vivid picture of Musa (a.s.), his early years, and the difficulties that he faced. There was a believer who hid his *iman* and believed in Musa (a.s.) when he returned to speak about Allah. He was a person who was always counselling Fir'awn and the people of Egypt to good. He would say to them, *My people! Think about the rationality of faith.*

You will find that the story of Fir'awn is a very direct example of the ones who are unwilling to receive Allah's mercy. They become unwilling to receive it by living a life of excess and sin, with arrogance and pride.

Allah then ends the *surah* with hope, and He invites us to be of those who worship Him. *Those who are resistant in making du'a and 'ibadah to me, they are the ones who are ultimately entering Jahannam.*

The next *surah* is Surah Fussilat, which means separation. In this *surah*, Allah speaks about the importance of the Qur'an and the ridicule that was laid upon the Prophet (s.a.w.). There is also a mention of the beautiful words of the Qur'an—that they are majestic on their own, and therefore the Prophet (s.a.w.) should be honoured as being its recipient.

Allah speaks about the Qur'an in very clear ways. It is a sign from Allah that bears good news. Allah gives evidence of it from the destruction of people who preceded us, who heard the scriptures and rejected them.

The believers are often mentioned in this *surah*. It speaks about them in terms of steadfastness. *Those who say our Lord is Allah, then remain steadfast. The angels descend upon them in this life and in the next life. Do not be scared nor have sorrow. You will always be given victory by Allah at the moment of life, in entrance into death, and into the next life.*

Allah also mentions about calling out to Him, worshipping and invoking Him. Allah also advises us, *Anytime that you have been given evil or rejection, return it with what is better than it.* Allah says that we can change a person on account of our good manners and our faith in Allah. He also invites us to be from those who seek protection from the *shaytan*. *When you recite the Qur'an, ask Me to protect you from the disturbance of the shayatin.*

Allah speaks about the unbelievers wanting to do *ilhad* with the Qur'an—to negate it, to not practise it, and to deal with it with frivolous disregard. Allah says that this is only at their own detriment.

Finally, He tells us about His creations, who He is, and why He has sent this book to us— that is, to make us the best human beings we can be. This is the closure of Surah Fussilat.

JUZ **25**

This *juz* begins with Surah Ash-Shura. Allah (s.w.t.) begins the *surah* by warning the people of Makkah and those surrounding it, as well as the rest of humanity, about the importance of the Qur'an. Allah says that He chooses whom He wishes to deliver the revelation to. Choosing Prophet Muhammad (s.a.w.) is not something that was accidental. It is not out of chaos, but out of choice. Allah has chosen him for a particular purpose. This is one of the places where we get one of the nicknames of the Prophet (s.a.w.) *Al-Mujtaba*—the selected one, the chosen one.

All of the prophets had the same call. Allah established that all of them called to *tawhid*. Allah then says that legal pathways in life are made different. What was sent to a previous messenger or a prophet may not be the same with what was sent to Prophet Muhammad (s.a.w.), and that should not surprise us.

Allah talks about the importance of being a person who consults and asks people for advice, *ash-shura*. The *surah* gets its name from this verse. *Your matters should always have a level of consultation.* A consultation that also goes past yourself and society, and especially with Allah is called *salatul istikharah*.

There is also the importance of *al-'afuw*. It means forbearance, clemency, and pardoning the errors and misjudgments of others. Not to be a person that cannot get past something that was done wrong to you in the past. Allah says that this is a noble characteristic of the Prophet (s.a.w.). It is one of those things that would always happen to a prophet, so they had to be able to forgive those who had done bad things in their past.

In the next section of the *surah*, Allah speaks about the Qur'an being something that is formative for the heart, the spirit, and the soul. There has to be this process where we allow the Qur'an to penetrate into our very being and to shape our character, actions, and dealings.

The next chapter is Surah Az-Zukhruf. It is a *surah* that begins with the reminder about the importance of the Qur'an. It opens with the letters *Ha Mim*.

Allah says that the Qur'an is a statement of the truth, and it is sent to end the debate with those who claim worship for other than Allah, those who have entered into the falsity of deifying other things. He also speaks about the argument that was put towards the Prophet (s.a.w.) in relation to those who were only following the practices of their forefathers and ancestors. They said to the Prophet (s.a.w.) that they could not leave the religion that had been practised by their people and within their culture for so many years, just on account of this new revelation. Allah says, *What good is holding on to something that was wrong if it was done wrong by those who came before you? They may not be as accountable as you are because they were not sent a messenger. But now you have heard the truth.*

Allah also determines each and every one of our shares in life. So do not have jealousy towards other people, and do not be proud and assume that you are the one who has brought everything into being for yourself. Both of them are issues of negligence and extreme behaviour that are disliked by Allah.

We are told about being on guard against evil, particularly the evil of bad company and friendship. In this *surah*, Allah gives the example of Fir'awn, who believed that his kingdom was a sign of his righteousness. *If I did not have this, then you may have a claim against me. But look! All the kingdom of Egypt belongs to me. Don't you see who I am?* That was used as evidence for him in his shallow mind that he was preferred by God—or in his mind, the deities.

Once again, Allah mentions about friendship. He says, *Those who advise you...* because Fir'awn had bad advisors who kept leading him on because of their own vested interests. Allah tells us to verify our friendship and to build this relationship based on *taqwa*.

Allah ends the *surah* by mentioning about the tragedy on the Day of Judgement. People who enter the Hellfire are going to call out to its guardian, Malik. *O' angel Malik, ask your Lord to put an end to us. We cannot take this anymore.* After a thousand years, Malik will respond, *You are going to remain in it for eternity.*

The next chapter is Surah Ad-Dukhan. It speaks about the blessing of the revelation of the Qur'an. It was revealed in a blessed month, on a blessed night, to a blessed prophet, and it is a blessed revelation and blessed book. Therefore, ask yourself what are the blessings of the Qur'an have you used in your life?

Allah speaks about life as being one that can lead you into sin and away from Allah if you follow your desires. Therefore, be on guard against the inner workings of your soul.

Arrogance is used as a theme in this *surah*; it destroys us just as it destroyed the people who came before us. The example given is Fir'awn. This is also the example given to the people of Quraysh. They are told not to rebel against the word of God.

At the end of the *surah*, Allah speaks about the punishment of the people in Jahannam and the reward of the people in Jannah. One of the most moving sections is the verse that says "*Indeed, the tree of zaqqum is food for the sinful.*" Its fruits are full of thorns and like the head of the devil.

The final *surah* of this *juz* is Surah Al-Jathiyah. It means to be brought down on your knees in humiliation. Allah speaks about His power as well as of the creations of the heavens and the earth and everything in between, and the things that we know of and what we never know of until He informs us or we are able to see it in the next realm.

Allah then speaks about the danger of being boastful and arrogant. You can see that this is a theme in the last three *surahs*. Allah tells us about that which hinders us from His path. It is that we desire to fulfil our lustful leanings, rather than to submit ourselves to Allah. One of the things that hinder us from submission to Allah is a bad company. *On the Day of Judgement, those who are going to be the worst enemies are those who were best friends in the dunya, except those who were best friends in piety and righteous conduct.*

The *surah* continues where Allah says that there is an enormous blessing in Allah accepting those who return from sin and push away against sin. Following our vain desires is only going to lead us further away from Allah.

This *surah* ends with the descriptions of the people of the Heaven and the people of the Hellfire, what it is that is necessary to be from the people of the Heaven, and what is needed to distance ourselves from becoming the people of the Hellfire. This book is a statement of truth that all praises are due to Allah, and we are to stay away from the signs of disbelief.

JUZ 26

This *juz* begins with Surah Al-Ahqaf. The opening of Surah Al-Ahqaf mentions the majesty of the creations of Allah (s.w.t.). Evidence of this is the intricacy of the heavens and the earth.

Allah speaks about the truthfulness of this revelation and the truthfulness of the one who had received it, Muhammad (s.a.w.). Allah also mentions the importance of parents in our lives, and He reminds us to be dutiful to them, not to dishonour them, and not to be from those who turn away from them unjustly.

Surah Al-Ahqaf is about the people of Hud (a.s.). Allah speaks about them being deprived of blessings that they would have received had they not strayed from the path of prophethood and prophecy. Therefore, you see that Allah ties our spiritual state with our material state.

It is one of the underlying themes of this *surah*. How you are with Allah also determines how you will be in terms of your contentment and prosperity.

Allah also mentions the *jinn*, an unseen creation. They are from those who are able to rationalise, understand, and follow the Qur'an as they are obligated to it. They were able to debate with the Prophet (s.a.w.), and after a sitting or two, they were able to accept the call. Some of them accept the truth, while others reject it.

The *surah* ends with Allah inviting us to be from those who have love of the Qur'an. It is a way of Allah (s.w.t.) inviting us to the truth of Jannah and its reality through our good conduct, and to protect ourselves from the punishment of the Day of Judgement. Eventually, there is compensation for those who are righteous, and there is retribution for those who are sinful.

Surah Muhammad, which is the next *surah*, is also referred to as Surah Al-Qital (The Warfare). Here, Allah (s.w.t.) speaks about the battle against the unbelievers in the time of the Prophet (s.a.w.). Allah says to stand up for that which is true and just, and do not turn your back away in fear.

In it are also contained the descriptions of rewards for the believers on the Day of Judgement, almost as if it is an inspiration. In contrast to that, it also speaks about the punishment that awaits the people lacking faith. Allah describes those who come away from the truth after knowing it as being people of desire, who follow their *hawwa*.

One of the special interest groups often mentioned in the *surah* is the hypocrites. Allah speaks about some of their traits. They turn away from battle when they should be defending truth, they spread mischief amongst the ranks of the believers, they turn away from pieces of evidence that were found in the Book and in the tradition as if they are deaf and blind to them, they do not pay attention to the statements of the Qur'an, they are from those who are willing to engage in the footsteps and follow the traps of the *shaytan*, and they have far-fetched fantasies and find it difficult to accept the realisation of the omnipotence of Allah. In the sum, they are those who have diseases in their hearts.

Allah also speaks about the power of the believers. Description of them comes in a very powerful way. Allah says that they are those who obey Allah, listen to Prophet Muhammad (s.a.w.), do not lose heart, are not weak or cowardly, and limit their disobedience of Allah even though they may have fallen prey to it at one point or another, and they are those who are rewarded fittingly by Allah on the Day of Judgement. Allah warns us at the very end of the *surah* that if we disobey Allah, He will replace us with a people who will not disobey Him.

The next *surah* is Surah Al-Fath (The Conquest). Here, Allah speaks about victory. It is a very hopeful and joyful *surah*. *Fear not, o' believers, the outcome is always going to be in favour of those who work righteous deeds and do that which is pleasing to Allah.*

Allah speaks about the blessing of faith and answering the concern of the believers. He also talks about the Treaty of Hudaybiyah and the incident related to it, where the Prophet (s.a.w.) made a pact with the *sahabah* under a tree to avenge 'Uthman (r.a.), who had been falsely claimed as having been killed by the Quraysh. Allah was pleased with the *sahabah*, and they were pleased with Him. That is the seal of approval to the pious and blessed generation of Prophet Muhammad (s.a.w.).

Surah Al-Fath ends with the mention of Prophet Muhammad (s.a.w.) and those who were with him. They are those who are strict in their fulfilment of the truth and pushing back against the aggression of the unbelievers. They are those who cohesively have mercy, humility, and compassion amongst them.

The following *surah* is Surah Al-Hujurat, which means the chambers. It refers to an incident where a man was calling out the name of the Prophet (s.a.w.)—they did not have the respect and etiquette that they should have had with the Prophet (s.a.w.). So Allah says, *Do not elevate your voice above the voice of the messenger, and do not be loud in your address to him the way you are with each other.*

The *surah* is about social ethics and social behaviours. It speaks about the importance of being careful with some of the great sins that a lot of people fall into: gossiping, backbiting, slandering, vilifying others, accusing others, and fighting with each other.

It speaks about having the characters of a believer. It speaks about the reprehensible nature of racism. It speaks about Allah guiding to faith those who seek it and those who turn to it with a pure heart.

With regard to our etiquette with the Prophet (s.a.w.), Allah tells us not to go to a place which the Prophet had not gone. This teaches us not to enter into *bid'ah*. We are not allowed to call out to him with rude statements.

Concerning general ethics, we should not mock each other, or pick faults with each other, or spy on each other, or use bad names and nicknames that the other person dislikes. We have to avoid backbiting and to be noble in the treatment of one another. At the end of it, Allah tells us to recognise that *the most virtuous of you in the sight of God is he who is righteous and has piety.*

The final *surah* of the *juz* is Surah Qaf. It speaks about signs that are found in this world. Allah speaks about different things like the heavens, the earth, the vegetation, the water, the dead land. He speaks about different prophets and people who preceded us: Nuh (a.s.), the people of Thamud, the people of 'Ad, Fir'awn, and Lut (a.s.). All of these are people and nations that are mentioned by Allah as evidence to us not to stray away from the path of truth.

Then Allah gives us the second part of the *surah*, which reminds us of our mortality. *The pain of death comes with its reality. Now I am going to be questioned.*

Allah ends the *surah* by letting us know that Jahannam will be filled, but we can escape it if we give our attention to the Qur'an by reciting and practising its teaching.

JUZ **27**

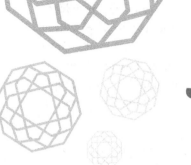

Juz 27 is in Surah Az-Zariyat. Allah makes a number of oaths to begin the *surah*. He makes an oath by the winds, the clouds, the ships that are able to sail in the seas, the angels, the Day of Judgement, and the creations of the heavens and the earth. Allah gives these as signs for God-fearing people.

Among the signs of the righteous is that they fulfil their prayers to Allah in the depth of the night—when others are asleep, they are awake. They are the people who pray for forgiveness, and they give the poor their right.

Allah gives an example of nations that came before us in the past. He tells us about Ibrahim (a.s.) and the guests that came to him, how he was informed that his wife would conceive, and how joyful she was. That was a miracle sent to him by Allah.

Allah speaks about Lut (a.s.) and the people of Sodom and Gomorrah, whom the angels were sent to destroy because of their excesses. He speaks about Fir'awn and Musa (a.s.), as well as the people of Thamud and the people of Nuh. All of them are signs from the people of the past, for the people of Quraysh and mankind, in general, to pay attention to.

Allah then mentions the purpose of life. *Neither the jinn nor mankind were brought into existence except for them to serve and to give their submission to Allah.* Everything that is created must fulfil that aim and purpose of worshipping Allah. That is the purpose of creation, and the wrongdoers therefore are those who do not understand it.

The next *surah* is Surah At-Tur. Allah speaks about the Mountain of Tur, which is where Musa (a.s.) received the revelation. It is a symbol for all the scriptures that were sent to humanity. There is also a reference to the populated house, *Al-Baitul Ma'mur*. A large number of angels come and make *tawaf* around it, and they never have an opportunity to return because there are always more angels waiting to honour and serve Allah.

Allah also says that no one can avenge or assist anyone that Allah has allowed to be in difficulty.

In the third section of the *surah*, Allah speaks about the Day of Judgement—how the sky will tremble, how the mountains will move and sway, how those who rejected faith will be forgotten while the people of Jannah will be celebrated and remembered by Allah.

Then Allah speaks about how He defends Prophet Muhammad (s.a.w.) from some of the false accusations that the people of Quraysh made against him. They said that the Prophet was a soothsayer, a mad man, and a poet. They said that he forged the Qur'an, and it is from his own tongue. Allah says, *Muhammad, keep your patience with Me and you will earn its reward.*

Allah then proclaims His purity as being distant from any of the false accusations that people had made about Him.

The next *surah* is Surah An-Najm. This *surah* has *sajdah* in it in the last verse. Here, Allah speaks about the signs of the Prophet (s.a.w.). He was not misguided, he does not speak from his own volition and desires, he had a meeting with the angel Jibril, and he was given the ascension to Allah.

Allah speaks about Sidratul Muntaha, which is a border in the heavens that the Prophet (s.a.w.) was able to cross when even angel Jibril could not. Allah speaks about the attitude of people who hear about these signs.

There will be those who disbelieve in them, but they are willing to believe in other ridiculous things like the pagan deities, Al-Lat, Al-'Uzza, and Manat. They follow their worldly desires when it is convenient, and they claim to not want to accept other things when it is inconvenient for them.

The ones who disbelieve in Allah are those who fall into the archaic belief of submitting to other than Him. The ones who believe in nothingness are also those who believe in something other than Allah. Allah speaks about the nations that were destroyed: 'Ad, Thamud, and others that came before them. It is because of their sinfulness that they were dealt with in that way.

The next *surah* is Al-Qamar. The moon was split, and it was a miracle of the Prophet (s.a.w.). On the Day of Judgement, the eyes will be humbled, people will be restrained, we will be like scattered moss in the wind, and everyone will be fearful for what will happen on that very difficult day.

The Qur'an is there for the advice that everyone needs to hear as to how to save themselves on that day. But who will give it their attention? In it, examples from previous nations are given—the people of Nuh, the people of Saleh, the people of Lut, the people of Musa, the people of 'Ad, the people of Thamud, Fir'awn and his people—nations that perished because of their unwillingness to accept the truth from Allah.

This *surah* ends as a transition into Surah Ar-Rahman. The virtuous who have heard the word of Allah will be seated in the seating of righteousness with Allah, and they will be honoured by Him.

Surah Ar-Rahman comes next. It is the only name of Allah that stands alone as an attribute that does not need explanation. Ar-Rahman is self-explanatory. He gives us the signs of His creations, the Qur'an, and the speech that He has blessed mankind with. The sun, the moon, the sky, the fruits, the dates, the trees, the creation of men and *jinn*, and so on—all of these are signs of His power. So do not disobey Him, and remember that the destruction of the world is in His Hand. You will be questioned, and He is not questioned. You are not able to penetrate past the barriers Allah has set. And Allah is in-charge of the heaven and the hell.

Allah speaks about the two destinations—the two gardens of the light. These are two gardens full of happiness in Jannah, for those who fear their Lord. Whereas for those who did not, they will be punished by Allah.

The gardens of Jannah are described as lush and green, with springs and fruits, date palms and pomegranates—full of happiness. All these different descriptions are similar to what we experience in the *dunya* as it is meant for us to understand the joy of it—not to say that they are the definitions.

Surah Ar-Rahman has one repeating verse: "*So which of the favours of your Lord would you deny?*" It is a question that you and I are to ask ourselves.

Surah Al-Waqi'ah comes soon after in this *juz*. It speaks about the calamity that befalls the Day of Judgement. The truth of the day is that everyone will be questioned, and everyone will experience it. There are three types of people: those who will be the foremost with Allah; the people of the right, who have done good deeds; and the people of the left, who have chosen the path of deviance. All of them will be given their reward or consequence by Allah.

Finally, Allah speaks about the creation of men, the creation of the seeds to become plants, the fire that is kindled by trees, and that Allah has destined things to cycle.

The very last *surah* is Surah Al-Hadid, and this is where the *juz* ends. It speaks about the attributes of Allah and the condition of the hypocrites on the Day of Judgement. There will be salvation and light for the believers, but none for the hypocrites. Also, in this *surah* is the verse that mentions iron being sent down upon the earth by Allah, which is geologically sound. ⬡

JUZ 28

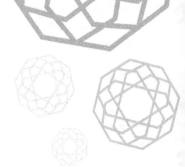

This *juz* is referred to as *Qad Sami'a*, which is the very first statements of the *juz*. Allah has heard the petition of the woman who has come to debate with the Prophet (s.a.w.).

Surah Al-Mujadalah begins with the legislation of *zihar*, which is when the husband treats his wife unfairly. Subsequently, Allah speaks about secretive consultations and discussions that isolate other people as being sinful behaviour. He speaks about the importance of obedience to our parents and obedience to our the Prophet (s.a.w.), and that there is no close friendship with people who disband from Allah, who seek to ridicule Allah and the Prophet (s.a.w.), or who seek to harm the believers. There are two clear parties in life: there is the party of *shaytan*, and there is the party of Allah.

The next *surah* is Surah Al-Hashr. It has many of the 99 names of Allah in it. It begins around the time of battle with some of the tribes that were rebellious against the Prophet (s.a.w.). They used to surround Madinah and fortified themselves, but Allah says that their fortification would not help them from Allah.

It speaks about the superior qualities of the *muhajirin*, who travelled to the Prophet (s.a.w.) and gave up everything to be with him, and of the *ansar*, who received the refugees from Makkah and the surrounding cities.

It also speaks about the traits of the hypocrites. They are those who make false commitments and who have a likeness to the *shaytan* in terms of their whispering. There are people for the Hellfire and there are people for Jannah. Both cannot be made equal.

Allah speaks about some of His characteristics and His divine names and attributes. Among them are Az-Zahir and Al-Batin, and He is The Apparent, The Unseen, The Merciful, The Compassionate, The King, The Owner of the Dominion, The Provider of peace and security, The Guardian, The Almighty, The Dominant, The Lord of all creations, The Creator, The Initiator, and He is The One of whom none is like Him.

The next *surah* is Surah Al-Mumtahinah. Instructions are made to believers, men and women, not to make close allies with those who are enemies. Allah gives the example of Ibrahim (a.s.); although he had a great fidelity, he disbanded from those who rejected God.

Allah speaks about testing the believing women that came to make *hijrah* to the Prophet (s.a.w.); if they would be willing and able to maintain what had been asked of them by Allah. Among the tests was that they must make a vow not to associate partners with Allah, not to steal, not to fornicate, not to commit infanticide and kill their children, not to slander, and not to disobey Allah and Prophet Muhammad (s.a.w.). The *surah* ends where Allah says, *You will not find anyone who has greater allegiance to Allah and His Messenger than the believers.*

The next *surah* is Surah As-Saf. It is about the best actions in the sight of Allah: to purify your intention for Allah, to do what Allah commanded, and to not be like the companions of Musa (a.s.) who used to harm him and make so many requests to him.

It speaks about the message that 'Isa (a.s.) conveyed to humanity, and foretold of the coming of the Prophet (s.a.w.), whom he referred to with the name *Ahmad*.

Allah talks about the best trade that a person can make with Allah, where they are willing to sacrifice their life and their wealth for that which is right, for the defence of those who are weak, and for the assistance of the weakest amongst the humanity. It speaks about the rewards of that trade: Jannah and happiness in this life. We are asked to be like those who were the true followers of 'Isa (a.s.), Al-Hawariyyin (the disciples).

Surah Al-Jumu'ah is one of those beautiful *surahs* where Allah speaks about the blessing and the weight of knowledge. The previous generations carried knowledge on their backs, but it is like a donkey carrying books, as they did not benefit from them. It asks us to be from those who are pure in insight and intention, in order for us to be able to access what Allah has revealed.

In Surah Al-Jumu'ah, there is an injunction to be from those who maintain the congregational prayers to leave off trade, commerce, and all distractions to come and answer that prayer every Friday at noon. That is what is blessed by Allah. Once that prayer is done, then go back to the *dunya* and seek from the bounties of Allah.

The next chapter is titled Al-Munafiqun, the hypocrites. Allah speaks about the incident of 'Abdullah ibn 'Ubay ibn Salul who was the chief of the hypocrites in the city of the Prophet (s.a.w.). He was of those who lied and gave false oaths, and he was very attractive in his speech, demeanour, position, and stature. Allah says,

Do not be confused with a person who appears well, that it means that their heart is alive and right. In the Qur'an, Allah condemns him and those who have a similar mindset.

Allah then advises the believers to stick to the firmness of faith and allegiance to the Messenger (s.a.w.) and to follow the tradition that leads us to Paradise.

The next *surah* is Surah At-Taghabun. Allah speaks about the day of gain and the day of loss, a reference to the Day of Judgement. He speaks about the purity of intention—to be a person whose intention is for Allah and is truthful with Allah, as that is the one saving grace for us on the Day of Judgement.

Allah speaks about the creation of man and the stories of those who came before us, as something that we can learn and benefit from. Then Allah talks about the day of gathering. It is the day when we will find those who have great success from those who have suffered the greatest loss. Those who are lost are those who have treated their wives and children as enemies in this life by not calling them to good, not praying with them, not being devout with them, and not leading them to that which is pleasing to Allah. Our children, our wealth, and our spouses are tests for us in this life. If we can pass it within our homes, then we can have security outside the home.

Allah also speaks about the merit of spending in the cause of God and being from those who are willing to bear the burden of society's needs.

The second last *surah* in this *juz* is Surah At-Talaq. It has many of the verses that relate to divorce, as well as some of the rituals and ethics of it. In this *surah*, Allah speaks about *taqwa*. That is a very intuitive and insightful point. Because one of the greatest things that happen at the time of divorce is that people forget Allah. They begin to act in a callous, hateful manner. So in this verse, Allah says for the ones who fear Him, He will give them an exit from all difficulties and sustenance from where they did not assume.

Allah speaks about the rulings of *'iddah*, the period of purity that stays after the moment of divorce, so that we can be sure that there is no paternity to result. He explains what the normal default is and what the rules and regulations of divorce are for those who do not get menstruation or for those who are pregnant.

Allah talks about the giving of provision and alimony for the women who are divorced and the children that may happen of it. Allah also speaks about the benefit of *taqwa,* as it is an overarching statement in all matters of life.

The very last chapter in this *juz* is Surah At-Tahrim. It is where Prophet Muhammad's wives made some comments to him that caused him to prohibit something lawful for himself, just to make them happy. Allah says to him, *O' Prophet, why do you make haram of what Allah has made halal for you? Is it to please your women?*

Allah then speaks about the virtues of repentance. He gives examples of righteous women and sinful women with their husbands. The immoral were the wife of Nuh (a.s.) and the wife of Lut (a.s.), while the righteous was the wife of Fir'awn. From there, you see that the wives of prophets were led astray, and the wife of a tyrant was led aright. And the *juz* finally ends with the example of Maryam (a.s.).

JUZ 29

This *juz* is referred to as Juz Tabarak, which is the first word of the first *surah* in the *juz*, Surah Al-Mulk. *Blessed and most elevated is Allah who in His Hand is all power and dominion.*

This *surah* speaks about the attributes of Allah. He is The Owner of all kingdoms, The Creator of life and death, The Creator of the heavens and the earth, The One who puts the stars where they are in the heavens, The One who has created the expanse that we enjoy in life.

Allah then speaks about those who disbelieve in Him and how they will be questioned on the Day of Judgement. Once they see the Hellfire and once they hear its terrible sound, they will be questioned, *Didn't a messenger come to you?* They will admit it and say, *Yes we had people who came and reminded us, but we were the ones who chose to stray from the truth.*

Allah speaks about the earth and its provisions, and the punishments that are set in as a balance to the corruption that people have caused on the earth. So if you live a clean life and have faith in Allah, you are from those who will be given from the kingdom of Allah. If you choose not to, then you might still be given the kingdom of the world but be deprived of the kingdom of Allah in the coming life.

In Surah Al-Qalam, Allah speaks about the truthfulness of His Messenger, Muhammad (s.a.w.). The *surah* begins with the letter *Nun* and an oath on the pen, which is to show us the significance of the pen and the importance of learning.

The Prophet (s.a.w.) was not a person of lewd character, or insane, or a soothsayer, or a criminal; he was not someone who had ever been ridiculed by anyone previously in the society. *Why did you start to ridicule him when he came to call you to purity?* Allah discusses the qualities of the disbeliever. They were unwilling to hear, to open their heart, or to allow a person to speak and provide that insight from the Prophet (s.a.w.).

Allah speaks about the massiveness of the Day of Judgement. How will it be for those who rebel against the truth? Allah says that He has given respite to people in this worldly life who adjust themselves and come back to the truth. But if they do not come to their senses, eventually Allah (s.w.t.) will hold all accountable. At the very end of the *surah*, Allah calls us to patience and perseverance in the face of atrocity.

The next *surah* is Surah Al-Haqqah (The Calamity). It mentions the reality of calamity of the Day of Judgement as what had happened to people in the past. The story of the people of Thamud, the people of 'Ad, Fir'awn and his people, and the people of Nuh are all shared. These are the people who were destroyed by Allah in what were considered natural occurrences, but these occurrences were commanded by Allah because of these people's sinfulness. Then Allah says that this is the punishment of the *dunya*, but what awaits them in the *akhirah* is more worrisome.

The Day of Judgement is a day of reckoning. There will be a blast and heralding for it. The people of the right and the people of the left will be separated.

The next *surah* is Surah Al-Ma'arij, means the ascent and the staircase. To ascend to Allah is a mammoth task. Allah says that the Day of Judgement is 50,000 years long. The skies will be dredged and the mountains will be like blown pieces of fabric and wool scattered in the wind. There will be no friendship on that day, except in matters of piety. People will run away from all of their family and loved ones, seeking protection from others, making claims against one another for having harmed them.

Allah speaks about the torments of the Hellfire, and He also speaks about the attributes of a weak man in comparison to the attributes of a righteous man. A weak man is the one who is weakened in his constitution, in his soul, in his desires. Whereas a man of strength and righteousness is a man of patience, endurance, fidelity, and love.

The next chapter is called Nuh. Prophet Nuh (a.s.) was sent as a warner to his people. His message was to worship Allah alone—to free one's self from worshipping anything other than Him, in both public and private life. You are to be a person of substance and honouring to God and to be a person who conveys wisdom to others.

Nuh's wisdom is shown in this *surah*. He said to his people, *Worship your Lord—worship none but He. He will open the heavens with its charity upon you. Its rain will flood you with blessings. You will be a person who will be given strength, wealth, and children. Everything you ask for will be given. But if you disobey, that same rain will come in destruction.* The people rejected his calls, and therefore Nuh (a.s.) invited the destruction of Allah upon them.

Allah saved him and his followers from that region. They were transported by the ship to another place, where they could begin fresh in the path of Allah.

Surah Al-Jinn is the next *surah*. This is the *surah* that was revealed to the Prophet (s.a.w.) and his companions to describe the reality of the unseen world—that there are creations other than us human beings. As Muslims, we believe that there are other beings that are not within our tangible presence. This is one of the *surah*s that speak of them—that they have a rational intellect and that their creation is similar to ours but different. However, their obligations to worship Allah is the same. There are two types of *jinn*: the believers and the unbelievers. Both of them are accountable to Allah.

Surah Al-Muzzammil comes in and speaks about the very first day of revelation. The Prophet (s.a.w.) descended from the mountain shivering, and his wife wrapped him to comfort him. And Allah instructs him, *O' the one who wrapped himself! Stand up and worship your Lord.*

The next *surah* is Surah Al-Muddaththir. *O' the one who wrapped himself! Stand up and invite people to the truth.* It is as if Allah is saying that you will only invite people to the truth if your worship of Me is solid. *O' the one who wrapped himself! Go out and preach. And after you have ensured that your prayer is solid, teach other people to pray.* Both of them go hand in hand. To be a person who will be able to influence others, you yourself must be sure that you are good with Allah.

Allah speaks about the importance of *tartil*, the recitation of the Qur'an in a precise way, as taught to the Prophet by Jibril. *Tajwid* is essential in that regard. Allah also speaks about how the destruction of the earth is heralded and that the Day of Judgement will arrive. There are also more instructions on the night prayer and its importance. He speaks about giving extra voluntary worship towards Allah and spending for the sake of Allah.

The Day of Judgement is described, especially as it relates to an arrogant, vengeful person. Allah warns him of the punishment of the Hellfire and not to have that pride that deters us from having faith and humility before Allah.

Allah speaks about the people of the right, those who choose the right path and those of piety, as being different from the people who will be destroyed in the Hellfire, the ones who choose the deeds of immorality and to stray from the path of truth.

Surah Al-Qiyamah once again talks about the Day of Judgement, and about a person's final hours before death, when the soul reaches the throat as it exits the body. Allah then says that there will be no refuge from Allah, except with Him.

Allah also speaks about the instructions of the Prophet (s.a.w.) regarding the Qur'an, that there will be faces glowing with light and faces that are gloomy on the day they return to Allah.

The next *surah* is Surah Al-Insan. It speaks about the favours of Allah to humanity. He creates us from nothing, and He shows us the right way. Then Allah speaks about condemning the deniers of the truth—they will be shackled and entered into the fire. On the other hand, the believers will be given a beautiful drink from Jannah.

Allah describes that the qualities of the believers in Jannah: they fulfil their vows, they fear their Lord, they feed the hungry, and they are sincere to Allah. They will have gardens of bliss, they will be given silver vessels to drink from and hanging fruit to consume, and everything will be of delight for them.

The final *surah* in Juz 29 is Surah Al-Mursalat. Allah sends the heralding winds, and Allah makes an oath by the wind, by the clouds, by the angels, by the Day of Judgement, and by the destruction of earlier people. Allah makes an important statement about the creation of men out of nothing; the earth, the mountains, and the springs are all created by Allah, and they are of the greater creations than us. Therefore, we must ponder upon that which is inanimate around us as a reflection of Allah's creation of us.

JUZ 30

Juz 'Amma, which gets its name from the first word of Surah An-Naba', speaks about descriptions of the Day of Judgement, how to avoid its terror, and how to gain its prosperity by living with good ethics and staying away from bad characters.

Allah describes the Day of Judgement in Surah An-Naba', Surah An-Nazi'at, the end of Surah 'Abasa, Surah At-Takwil, and Surah Al-Infitar. All of these are the *surah*s with that theme. And Allah mentions ethics in Surah Al-Mutaffifin, Surah Al-Fajr, Surah Al-Balad, Surah Al-Layl, Surah Ad-Duha, and Surah Al-Ma'un. All of these *surah*s are about caring for the poor, caring for the elderly, feeding those in need, and looking after the orphans (especially in Surah Ad-Duha).

The primary theme of this *juz* is the early revelations that were sent to Prophet Muhammad (s.a.w.). They are typified by short verses with a very rhythmic resonance sound that is easy to remember. It is one of the reasons why it is the first section of the Qur'an that young students are encouraged to memorise.

The next section of this *juz* is about the importance of the Qur'an and its finality in the message that is sent by Allah as communication from Him to humanity. It is the final scripture. What it does is that it completes the favour of Allah upon humanity. It makes adjustments to what has been corrupted by the hands of men over time. It brings clear proof of its authenticity; a good example of which can be found through Surah Bayyinah in this *juz*.

Another section is the importance of purification and getting yourself ready for the challenge of life, giving your soul the necessary training so that it can become elevated and purified. *Surely those who are successful are the ones who elevate their soul and nurture it. And those who lose themselves on the Day of Judgement are the ones who overlook its importance.*

One of the main sections that you find established in this final *juz* of the Qur'an is about the story of the nations that perished before us. Surah Al-Fil talks about those to whom Allah sent little birds with pebbles to destroy them. All of these are about important principles sent by Allah, defending the believers, that sacrifice needs to be made, and that ultimately, those who go against God will be vanquished, brought to account on the Day of Judgement or destroyed in this worldly life.

Finally, there is a call to increase doing good deeds. Allah tells us to weigh our deeds, because they will be weighed for us. Surah Al-Zalzalah mentions that the one whose scale is heavy on the Day of Judgement will be from those who are blessed. And Surah Al-Qari'ah mentions that the one whose scale is not heavy with good deeds will have no goodness, and they will be bereft of all happiness.

The very first word of revelation, "*Iqra*", is found in this *juz* in Surah Al-Alaq, and we perform the *sajdah* in this *surah*. Allah gives us a solution to any difficulties in life, *Increase your prostrations to Me and grow close to Me, and you will find Me always with you.*

The *juz* ends with an acknowledgement of Allah's omnipotence and ability to give us good even in times of difficulty. Allah speaks of this in Surah Al-Kauthar. *O' Muhammad, I have given you an abundance of blessing. Therefore, give over your devotions, your sacrifices, and your rituals to Allah. The One who wages against you is going to lose that battle. You will always be on top if you remain with the truth.*

Another important *surah* near the end of this *juz* is Surah An-Nasr. This is one of the *surah*s that were revealed in Madinah, after the *hajj* of the Prophet (s.a.w.), around 80 days or so before his death. It was seen as a foreshadowing of the ultimate return of the Prophet (s.a.w.) to Allah. The victory of Allah is that Islam will continue to spread. *O' Muhammad, nothing is left for you to do in this mission, except to be thankful to Allah, praising of Him, and asking for His forgiveness and mercy.*

The other four most notable chapters all begin with the word *Qul*. Surah Al-Kafirun, which starts with "*Qul ya ayyuhal kafirun*", is equal to a quarter of the Qur'an. By that, it means the knowledge contains within it is equal to one out of every four things that the Qur'an speaks about, which is separating between truth and falsehood and giving people an opportunity to come to faith—for those who do not want to, it is up to them. *I will never worship what you worship falsely. Unless you come truly to faith, we do not need the hypocrisy that you pretend to believe in what I believe.*

The last three *surah*s are very important. Surah Al-Ikhlas illustrates sincerity and seeking only God. It is one of the *surah*s that is first memorised by all Muslims. *Say, He is Allah, The One.* He is not one because there is a second to him. He is One because there is no one that is like Him. He is The One that everyone relies on. He did not emerge, and nothing has come from Him in that sense. He does not have a son and He was not begotten. And there is nothing that is similar to Him. Anything conceived, imagined, or thought of could never be like the reality of our Creator, The Almighty Allah.

The last two chapters of the Qur'an are known as *Al-Mu'awwizatayn*. You can see their distinction as the Prophet (s.a.w.) used them as a *ruqyah*, spiritual healing. The Prophet (s.a.w.) said that for any ailment, fear, or distress that we have in life, these two *surahs* are sufficient and will suffice us. So it is something that we should regularly recite to protect ourselves and our families. It is as if Allah is protecting us in both *surahs*, altogether totalling 11 verses. They protect us from both the spiritual and the material things that bother us, from whatever ails you in your heart—the whispering of the shaytan, the feeling of depression, sorrow, and angst, the unseen forces, and also the human beings.

The very last word of the Qur'an is *An-Nas*. If you are able to look at the beginning of the Qur'an till the end, you will see it begins with Allah making us a promise. *You are asking, O' Allah, lead us to the straight path*, and Allah says, *If you continue to pray until the very end, you will be from those of mankind who are saved.* ❁

NOTES

NOTES

NOTES

NOTES

NOTES